The Stripping of
the Altars

Professor MacKinnon, as Norris-Hulse
Professor of Divinity in the University of
Cambridge, is primarily concerned with the
philosophy of religion. Before coming to
Cambridge in 1960 he was for thirteen years
Regius Professor of Moral Philosophy in
the University of Aberdeen, and earlier still
he taught in the universities of Oxford and
Edinburgh. He has been a Gifford Lecturer
in the University of Edinburgh and has held
numerous other lectureships in universities
about the country. His interests are now con-
centrated on fundamental problems on the
frontiers of philosophy and theology. His
inaugural lecture in Cambridge, *The
Borderlands of Theology,* he used also as the
title of a volume of essays, published last
year, and more perhaps than any other
formula it conveys the central direction of
his intellectual engagement.

By the same author

A STUDY IN ETHICAL THEORY
published by A. & C. Black

BORDERLANDS OF THEOLOGY
published by Lutterworth Press

also in Fontana Books

GOD, SEX AND WAR
Edited by D. M. MacKinnon

DONALD M. MacKINNON

The Stripping of
the Altars

The Gore Memorial Lecture
delivered on 5 November 1968
in Westminster Abbey,
and other papers and essays
on related topics

COLLINS

THE FONTANA LIBRARY
THEOLOGY AND PHILOSOPHY

First published in the Fontana Library 1969

© 1969 D. M. MacKinnon

Printed in Great Britain
by Richard Clay (The Chaucer Press), Ltd.,
Bungay, Suffolk

Contents

Introduction

The lecture which introduces this volume was delivered as the Gore Memorial Lecture in Westminster Abbey on 5 November 1968. The version spoken in the Abbey was somewhat shorter than the one which is now published.

It may seem improper for one whose primary concern is the philosophy of religion, to venture into the field of ecclesiology. But the crisis of belief through which we are living, and of which I am professionally aware literally every day, inevitably affects and is affected by the actual situation of the Churches. Thus the weary archaism of the present establishment of the Church of England distorts and inhibits a properly existential realization of the actual, present *Sitz im Leben* of the Christian community, of its perils and its opportunities. But this is only one palmary instance of the way in which those involved in ecclesiastical structures cling obstinately to the fading memory-image of a position they once enjoyed, failing altogether to meet the realities of a post-Constantinian situation.

It is a common theme of these essays (for all their diversity) that the Churches are in this present emerging from the age of Constantine, emerging from the tunnel of the experience which began with that emperor's adherence to the Christian faith. To use a seeming pejorative such as tunnel is to suggest an almost philistine disregard for the achievements of Christendom in the domains of culture and of human civilization. Yet it remains a tragic fact that for those glories a terrible price was paid. From

Caesar the Church of Christ learnt to speak with the accents of Caiaphas, learnt how often it was expedient that one man should die for the people, how often it was a luxury to be indulged only by the irresponsible to leave the ninety and nine sheep in eager quest for the wayward stray.

Or if the Church refrained from making those accents those of its own speech, it deliberately abdicated from the task of criticizing the methods adopted by allegedly responsible, human authorities, finding in acceptance rather than in protest, in obedience rather than revolt, the discipline of a somewhat macabre *via crucis* for its members. Always there was the tacit assumption that the ways of government were the ways of God: because, by (presumably) the most damaging anthropomorphism of all Christian intellectual history, the creator and governor of the world had been invested with the quality of an absolute, human ruler, the savage exactions of a Henry VIII (to take one extreme example) were received as parables of the Lordship of him who was among men as their servant.

We live in a radically democratic age, in which established sanctities are ceaselessly called in question, compelled to justify their claim by reference to the human values they promote. The temper of this protest is often crudely utilitarian, unaware of the serious criticisms to which a thoroughgoing utilitarianism in ethical theory is open (whether 'rule-utilitarianism' or 'act-utilitarianism' is in mind); but the demand which thus finds expression is the fundamentally healthy rejection of an order which secures certainly a measure of respect for certain traditional values, but only at the cost religiously of a profound deformation of the ultimately radical faith of the incarnation through its conversion into the underlying spiritual tradition of a supposedly supremely excellent civilization.

In such a situation it is always tempting for the Christian to espouse the cause of conservatism, not in the narrowly political, but in the broadly cultural sense. The very weight of historical experience encourages on the part of the Churches a collective bias in favour of their inherited securities. And of no Church is this more true than the Church of England. That Church certainly has her radicals; but sometimes (not always) they combine a tendency to treat questions relating to the historical foundations of their faith as irrelevant to its substance, with an obstinate, ecclesiological fundamentalism.[1] Jesus becomes virtually a variable to whom it is possible to assign as values whatever likeness a favoured tradition of public and private devotional practice may crave. But this (to my mind intellectually intolerable) detachment from fundamental questions of belief is made possible and compensated by a deep, unyielding commitment to the historical forms of institutional, ecclesiastical existence. So one is told that for the faithful clergy and laity in an English diocese to choose their chief pastor could only lead to 'chaos'. But what is this chaos? Might it not be the chaos out of which a new, more objectively significant form of Christian presence to the modern world was fashioned? More profoundly we have to ask ourselves whether by our conservatism we may not be seeking to quench the spirit of God, leading the Churches towards a new birth which must touch the most fundamental forms of their existence.

To emerge self-consciously, and in a spirit of acceptance (and I do *not* mean by this, endorsement of the

---

[1] For instance, questions relating to the manner in which Jesus conceived his mission and approached his death. Cf., for example, the theology of John Knox.

standards of a so-called 'permissive society'), into the light of the post-Constantinian age; to seek the forms of post-Constantinian existence *both in respect of inter-Church relations and in respect of presence to the world*; to purge out of the collective and private imaginations of Christian people the last vestiges of their eagerness to approach the believer *de haut en bas*; to welcome the many possibilities opened in a new situation radically to rethink such ethical problems as those raised by the methods of modern warfare and by men's rapidly extending mastery over their environment; (most fundamentally) to liberate our basic theology from the inherited infection of centuries of acquiescence in an objectively false situation *vis-à-vis* public authority—these are the imperatives, and these the opportunities of the post-Constantinian world. We live in an age in which faith (and the institutional forms in which that faith is expressed) must be tested to destruction. It is tempting to seek to avoid that testing by numbing the sharpness of the challenge to faith, and expending every energy to conserve as an archaic enclave in the modern world the highly questionable structures in which Christian practice and belief were previously expressed. Let the structures go, and the confrontation becomes inexorable; yet that way is also the way of promise. It is as a contribution to various aspects of this crucial discussion that these essays are collected together.

One paper—that on 'Theology and Tragedy', which appeared in *Religious Studies* in 1967—stands rather by itself. In the Gore Lecture I refer to Plato's treatment of tragedy; I thought therefore that some readers might care to consult in connection with this section of the lecture an essay in which I endeavoured to bring out the significance of that criticism, and the consequences of the unconscious readiness of Christian theological tradition to endorse it.

Inevitably some of these papers overlap; for, written, delivered or broadcast, they represent concern with the same problems. It is impressive that two of them, completed in November 1967 and in November 1968 respectively, pay tribute to Father Robert Adolfs's book—*The Grave of God: Has the Church a Future?* I know I am not alone in finding in that small volume one of the truly prophetic works of recent years. If by my writing I can encourage Anglicans, especially those theologians who combine a *soi-disant* theological radicalism with an ecclesiological conservatism, and those who occupy positions of authority and decisive influence in the existing ecclesiastical structure, to apply its lessons to the evaluation of the alleged inheritance to which in various ways with various emphases they cling so resolutely, I shall not have written in vain. I would venture to hope also that those who already know Father Adolfs's book, and share my admiration and gratitude for it, may find the occasional valuable development, or even correction, of some of his themes in the pages that follow; I could imagine no greater tribute to this small book.

D. M. MACKINNON

Cambridge
21 December 1968

Kenosis and Establishment

'All this line of thought—all this way of conceiving of God's self-restraining power and wisdom—at least prepares our mind for that supreme act of respect and love for His creatures by which the Son of God took into Himself human nature to redeem it, and in taking it limited both His power and His knowledge so that He could verily live through all the stages of a perfectly human experience and restore our nature from within by a contact so gentle that it gave life to every faculty without paralysing or destroying any.'[1]

These words occur towards the end of Charles Gore's most sustained study of the conception of *kenosis* and I quote them at the outset of this memorial lecture in that it is with aspects of the notion of *kenosis* that I am mainly concerned. It is also appropriate to quote from this essay in particular in that it was written during the period in which its author was a residentiary canon of this Abbey Church. I wish, however, to follow the quotation from Gore's essay with another more extended quotation, this time from a remarkable book by a Dutch Augustinian prior, Father Robert Adolfs, entitled in the English translation *The Grave of God: Has the Church*

[1] *Dissertations on Subjects Connected with the Incarnation*, by Charles Gore, M.A., Canon of Westminster; Superior of the Community of the Resurrection, Radley. Published by John Murray, London, 1895; p. 224.

a Future?[2] The chapter from which I quote is significantly entitled 'The Church and Kenosis':

'What we are now experiencing is the Church's coming of age, her maturity. She *had* to follow this "wrong way" in order to come to a better and deeper understanding of herself and her mission. The Church has not wasted time or trouble in following the wrong ways that I have referred to. She has not simply wandered aimlessly around. She has had to follow this way (of suffering) in order to achieve greater spiritual maturity.

'In the parable of the prodigal son, the father does not try to restrain his son when he wishes to set out on his journey. The son's road reaches a dead end, but he *returns* inwardly mature and with even greater love for his father, to the "origin" of his way, to the original parting of the ways. He will set out once more, but greatly enriched by all that he has experienced on the other way. He has not broken the link with his father. On the contrary, this link is greatly strengthened.

'In the same way, the Church has not lost the inheritance of Christ on her "wrong way". She has not broken the link with grace. She too can set out again, enriched by her experience and purified by suffering. Her new way must be a genuinely Christian way. Does it exist for the Church? I believe that it does, and I have called it the way of *kenosis*.'

The whole chapter from which these words are a quotation merits the closest study and represents an extremely bold and encouraging extension of the concept of *kenosis* to the field of ecclesiology. Father Adolfs is of

[2] E. T. by D. N. Smith, published by Compass Books, Burns & Oates, London, 1967; p. 109.

course a Roman Catholic, and he writes primarily for members of that communion; but the lessons which he seeks to enforce both here and elsewhere in his book are of nearly universal significance. The boldness of his argument is a most impressive example of the way in which in the present ferment in the Roman Church men and women are learning lessons of the greatest possible significance for the whole of Christendom. Father Adolfs applies the image of the prodigal's residence in the far country to characterize in a single, comprehensive, devastating and extremely illuminating picture vast tracts of the Church's history from the conversion of Constantine until the present day. One is tempted to suppose that in his heart he more than half agrees with that friend of Charles Gore, Father R. M. Benson, the founder of the Society of St John the Evangelist, that the conversion of Constantine was the greatest single disaster ever to overtake the Christian Church. Certainly, and here I can only express myself in heart-felt agreement with his underlying conviction, Adolfs regards the advent of the post-Constantinian age of the Christian Church as a period of unexampled opportunity as well as of severe testing; unexampled opportunity in that it opens the doors wide to a new reformation in which the radical spirits in his own Church of Rome are among the foremost participants.

In the passage that I have quoted he sketches the outline of a philosophy of Church history, seeing the age which is ending as a necessary stage in the Church's progress to maturity; many will agree with me that he puts too bland a construction on a long history of compromise and betrayal. But it is hard to have anything but the greatest admiration for the way in which he finds in the notion of *kenosis* one of the key ideas required for the renewal of the Church's understanding of its mission.

Historically, as the quotation from his dissertation 'On the Consciousness of our Lord' well illustrates, the use of the notion of *kenosis* in the field of Christology will always be associated with Gore's memory and it is therefore surely appropriate in 1968 to build a lecture intended to commemorate his work around the contemporary significance of that idea, even extending its scope to the sharp criticism of assumptions to which Gore remained in bondage throughout his life. If, however, I express myself in these terms in agreement with Father Adolfs, I know that I must scrutinize as strictly as I can assumptions by which I have myself often been guided.

What Father Adolfs is pleading for is, in the first instance, a renewal of understanding of the manner of the Church's presence to the human societies in which its work is carried on; but he recognizes quite clearly that this touches also the nature of its self-understanding, and indeed the way in which it understands its mission and the faith by which its existence is defined. So he latches on to the idea of *kenosis* or self-emptying (a much criticized but, in my judgment, a crucially significant Christological concept) and urges its application in the field of ecclesiology at once in theory and in pastoral practice. Certainly the notion of *kenosis* as a Christological concept has been drastically criticized. Thus in his admirable Hulsean Lectures, *The Divinity of Jesus Christ*,[3] the late Professor J. M. Creed insisted that the conception of a depotentiated Logos involved in the theory as he understood it, seemed to carry quasi-mythological suggestion of a very doubtful character. He did not see how it could be supposed that the Lord abandoned his cosmic functions for the period of the incarnation or even within the sphere of the incarnate life withheld himself from their exercise. And there are other grave criticisms.

[3] Reprinted in the Fontana Library, 1964.

Such paradoxes in the theory are well known. Yet I would plead for it that it calls attention not only to what is suggested by Paul's words in Philippians 2 and elsewhere, but also to the unfaltering stress of the fourth Gospel on the Son's dependence on the Father, on an authority affirmed because of and in the context of a supreme humility, an 'infinite self-abnegation', in Dean Inge's phrase. If this authority is found intolerable, it is because of the indirection of its manifestation; we do not find it unbearable in the way in which we find unbearable the exercise of ecclesiastical authority either in the manner of the more intransigent officers of the Roman Church in the months following the publication of the papal encyclical *Humanae Vitae*, or in that characteristic of the kind of English bishop who graduates to the episcopal bench from the headmastership of an English public school. Further, the concept of *kenosis* advertises the relevance of the costliness of the incarnate life to the absolute. If one cares, so to speak, it raises again the issue of divine impassibility by asking what light, if any, the manner of the ministry and passion of Jesus throws upon the being of the divine in itself, and on the nature of its relation to the created world. We have already said that it puts a question-mark against much of the manner and exercise of ecclesiastical authority. The career of the rabbi of Nazareth does not suggest that of a Roman curial cardinal, or that of the headmaster of an English public school.

The notion of *kenosis* dares to carry back into the initiating act of the whole incarnate life that which is qualitatively similar to what it manifested. 'There was a Calvary above which was the mother of it all.' It has, moreover, deep relevance to the articulation of the doctrine of an essential as distinct from an economic Trinity. Further, the extension of the concept to the field of

ecclesiology enables us to achieve deeper perception concerning its primary Christological significance. When the
concept is so extended, it is extended to a field in which
acknowledgment of the unity of theory and practice becomes inescapable. It is arguable that some at least of the
antinomies which we encounter in developing the concept Christologically are due to the extent to which our
total understanding of the relation of God to man is
obscured by the radically distorted image presented in
and by the institution supposed to convey its sense to the
world. When the significance of *kenosis* for ecclesiology is
boldly grasped, when, for instance, such concepts as ministry and apostolate are thought through in accordance
with its implications, its fundamental Christological
sense may well receive drastic illumination.[4]

All this sounds excessively abstract; but one can bring
it down to earth very sharply, even poignantly. Theological progress may be dependent on the criticism of the
Church's institutional experience, even the rejection of
long tracts of that experience as fundamentally invalid.
In such criticism may well lie the necessary condition of
really fundamental theological progress. Yet the liberating dynamic of a purely theological idea may itself be
among the initial conditions of such criticism. I say that
it may be among those conditions; I am equally sure that
they will also include precisely the sort of changes in the
sociological position of the Church that Father Adolfs
indicates. He wrote with his own Roman Catholic
Church in mind; I speak against the background of a
very vivid sense of the decline in prestige and influence of
the Anglican Communion, with my mind filled also by a
sense of the presently precarious situation of Christian

---

[4] On the subject of *kenosis* in Christology, see my forthcoming
Prideaux Lectures, delivered before the University of Exeter in 1966.

belief. I can only speak with any sort of authority if I admit that I speak as an intellectual, as one who is professionally preoccupied with issues of validity, of truth, of verification. Yet these issues pressed most certainly on Gore's mind and the attempted *magnum opus* of his retirement, we recall with admiration, was entitled *The Reconstruction of Belief*. It may be judged a failure; but we must admire the temper of a man who saw the cruciality of the issues with which he sought to deal. If I am right, the idea of *kenosis* is precisely one of the potentially liberating theological ideas of the present, one of the ideas that may help towards a reconstruction, I will not say of belief, but of the presentation—I would myself like to say the 'system of projection'—of the proximate object of belief.

I turn now, in the light of what I have set out in general terms, to comment critically on various types of fundamentalism which stand in the way of the sort of renewal the present not only demands but seems to make possible. I use the word fundamentalism advisedly; for it is most important that we should realize that the fundamentalist temper is by no means exclusively expressed in terms of an adherence to belief in the supposed verbal inspiration of the Scriptures. There are, indeed, many sorts of fundamentalism—ecclesiological and liturgical, to mention two at least as deadly in their way as the more familiar biblical variant.

It was remarked by the Bishop of St. Andrews, Dunkeld and Dunblane,[5] in an article published in the October number of *Scan*, the monthly newspaper of the Episcopal Church in Scotland, that the Lambeth Conference of 1968 might be regarded as the swan-song of traditional

[5] Dr Howe.

Anglo-Catholicism. The judgment was an interesting one, and the fact that it was made encourages me to continue the development of my theme by reference to the presence in that tradition of a temper which, if it cannot be condemned out of hand as imperialistic, none the less embodies in living and destructive form something of the spirit of apartheid.

When he became bishop of Worcester (according to the obituary in *The Times*), Gore resigned from the English Church Union, the Confraternity of the Blessed Sacrament, etc.: this because he judged membership of such partisan societies incompatible with the obligations of the episcopal office. But throughout his subsequent career, for all his deep differences with the policy of the Anglo-Catholic party over such matters as the extra-liturgical cultus of the Blessed Sacrament, he remained in the public mind identified with that attitude of rigorously exclusive superiority towards members of non-episcopal churches which has been perhaps the most sheerly destructive element in the Anglo-Catholic inheritance. It is worth recalling Gore's attitude in a lecture on the ecclesiological import of *kenosis*, inasmuch as it would be hard to conceive any attitude more totally alien to an attempted expression in institutional terms of *kenosis* as of the *esse* of the Church, and as something supremely indicative of its apostolicity.

A future historian may well say that this evil temper (for so it must be characterized) was endemic in the Tractarian movement and the successive failures of the Anglo-Catholicism which succeeded it from the first. He may also say that it reached its cruellest expression in the venomous and obsessive campaign, coinciding to no small extent with the years of the last war, over the adherence to the projected Church of South India of the Indian dioceses in that country.

This episode still awaits detailed analysis by a historian, an analysis which must not shrink from anathematizing the curious mixture of imperial patronage and English parochialism that marked its underlying judgment on the developing pattern of Indian Christianity. It will also require something of the sensitivity of the tragic poet to portray the sad scandal of religious men and women bound by the traditional three-fold vows of the religious life, turning in a time of war and terror from the promotion of a spirit of peace to the sowing of seeds of bitter and destructive controversy. No one who is familiar (as I am) with the writings and spiritual teaching of such men as the late Father W. B. O'Brien, S.S.J.E., the superior of the Cowley Fathers at that time, or of the late Dom Gregory Dix, will question the great services that these men did not only to the Church but also to many individuals; they were men of the greatest spiritual depth. One must therefore call it tragic that they so bent their energies at that time to the service of the harshest and most intransigent bigotry. It is also unfortunately true that they received a large measure of backing from the most distinguished theologian on the episcopal bench at that time, Dr Kenneth Escott Kirk, Bishop of Oxford, whose Bampton Lectures on *The Vision of God* is one of the greatest works of Anglican theology in this century. If one says that these men did great damage, one does no more than point out what is involved in seeing something genuinely tragic in their behaviour. It is no answer to say that great principles were at stake. Issues of truth are obscured by the weapons men and women use to fight them. Of the spirit manifested in that episode one's verdict must be that it bore no mark at all of that manner of concern for ultimate truth on which, in the Christian's understanding of the Church's Lord, the Father has set his seal: I mean that witness to the truth which no more relies on the compulsive power of superior propaganda than it does on that of physical force, but which leaves the issue open, and is receptive, expectant, always seeking to fulfil the law of self-emptying, of *kenosis*. The word I would emphasize in that last sentence is the word receptive. An authentic Christian fidelity to tradition is always receptive, ready to learn, open to promise.

Yet what was seen writ in large letters in the bitter agitation over the Church of South India was a temper which had already, by its arrogance, inflicted damage in untold cases at a more personal level. I am not thinking, as those who hear or see these words may suppose, simply of the way in which individual priests have resisted any and every suggestion and resolution of the Convocations or the recommendations of successive Lambeth Conferences to admit to Communion non-Anglicans who have not received episcopal confirmation; such episodes are indeed deplorable. But I refer to the attitude of mind which has continually queried the authenticity of the ministry of the non-episcopally ordained, and in particular of their sacramental practice. It is not the 'fencing in' of the Anglican altar that I have in mind; rather it is the refusal to develop a concept of the authentically Christian (I am trying to avoid such over-worked terms as orthodoxy and validity) which will encourage without sacrifice of that which is supposed to be precious truth, a readiness to permit the way in which that truth has been received to win enlargement from those who stand within a seemingly alien tradition. There is an issue here ultimately of spirituality; but it is also one that touches what to an intellectual must lie near the heart of the matter, namely the manner of receiving and understanding the mysteries of faith. There is offence in the older attitude not only against the claims of charity but also against those of truth.

But how may a man receive that which seems to contradict what he believes? What is the paradigm and model of enlargement with which we must work? Is it one that allows the fragmentariness of our perceptions to stand in need of correction, or is it one that is unselfconsciously committed to the assumption that the Incarnate was in simple sense, omniscient and endowed his apostles with a comparable infallibility of insight? We must reject the latter assumption categorically on Christological grounds. For surely the manner of Christ's ministry imposes on us the need to reconstruct altogether the concept of the divinity predicated of Christ, and our concepts of the attributes whereby we suppose the unity of that divine nature anatomized. Some such demand was made admittedly by kenoticists of different schools; and here I include Peter Taylor Forsyth, as well as the Charles Gore whose essay I quoted at the outset of this lecture, his friend Henry Scott Holland, and their successor in the development of the kenotic idea, Frank Weston, Bishop of Zanzibar. We need to continue their work and find in it the source of ethical illumination that in the essay quoted from his *Dissertations* Gore clearly thought we might find. It is indeed as a contribution to the extended use of the concept in the field of ecclesiology that this lecture is offered.

A little while ago I referred to the many varieties of fundamentalism. In the volume *The Apostolic Ministry,*[6] which has recently been reprinted in a new edition, we have a nearly classical case of the spirit of ecclesiological fundamentalism. But the proper corrective to all fundamentalism lies in a more profound theology, and where

[6] Edited by the late Dr K. E. Kirk and published by Hodder & Stoughton, 1946.

theology is concerned, Christology is for the Christian its key.

'He that hath seen me hath seen the Father,' Jesus said, according to St John, who also said in the same Gospel, 'I and the Father are one [thing]', and further, my Father is greater than I'. These sayings, set in the mouth of the Lord by one of his most profound interpreters, put to the theologian the task of reconstructing the concept of identity involved in the second logion so as to avoid its apparent contradiction with the third. To pose the question in terms of the logical compatibility of two propositions, and the avoidance of the counter-intuitive consequences of asserting both of them, has a very old-fashioned ring. Yet the demand made is one which, if we seek to fulfil it, involves us sooner or later in the most radical criticism of all our fundamentalisms. *Indeed, such a criticism is a condition of successful reconstruction.* We seek a certain internal consistency in our concepts and if we achieve it then our logical analysis precipitates us into criticism of any attempt to establish a security for ourselves by allowing as unauthenticated other roads for which surely room must be found on a proper map of the way of faith. It is not the exaltation of autonomy in the abstract which brings down our most treasured idol; it is learning that receptivity belongs to God as he is in himself. And we must say that receptivity does belong to God as he is in himself, if we deny that Christ is a mere simulacrum of the divine but rather insist that in him we have 'God's presence and his very self and essence all divine'. His invitation to the outcast is not adequately seen as a mere parable of the divine invitation, but rather as its *actuality* become event.

One notices today a tendency in Christological discussion to quote with admiration the remark of Professor

John Knox: 'The divinity of Jesus was the deed of God. The uniqueness of Jesus was the absolute uniqueness of what God did in him.' The confusion of categories wantonly made in Knox's first proposition offends me as a philosopher; what is even more disquieting is the extent to which his vaguely disguised Adoptionism is commended as a valuable contribution to the development of the doctrine of Christ's person. In the statements made in this section of the lecture it will be seen that I am committed Christologically to complete acceptance of the *homoousion*. It is indeed in the strength of this commitment that I am urging the sort of resolute reformation of ecclesiological assumptions I believe to be implied by recognition that in the rabbi of Nazareth we discern the ways of God as he is in himself.

The sort of radical reformation of ecclesiastical styles for which I am pleading in this lecture is immensely easier for us in that we have entered the post-Constantinian age. The deadly evils which characterized the Anglo-Catholicism of the early 'forties which I have mentioned (and they were deadly evils and are such still where they remain) are of course part of the built-in inheritance of the Constantinian Church, the Church whose status is guaranteed and which allows the manner of that guarantee (the exercise by the civil power of a measure of external compulsive authority) to invade the substance of her life. The temper of exclusion encourages men to think of membership of Christ's Body after the manner of the claim *civis Romanus sum*. In Anglo-Catholicism it was a claim that by such membership men stood at the heart and centre of history and thus, after the likeness of a sharply exclusive citizenship, were the superiors of all lesser breeds without the law. In the complexities of Anglican history, we know also that such attitudes have had, where relations with the Free Churches are con-

cerned, a certain continuing confirmation through the
social position of the Church of England. Too often
Establishment has been a ground for boasting rather than
an opportunity for presence; a status ensuring a counter-
feit security rather than a way of assuring that there shall
be no withdrawal from the actualities of human life.

May I turn to another related but more general topic?
'The end justifies the means': so Caiaphas, when he gave
counsel, that it was expedient that one man should die
for the people, 'that the whole nation perish not'. It is not
enough to dismiss his argument as that of a hard *Real-
politiker* governed by *raison d'état*, eager to preserve the
theocracy. The danger he foresaw was real enough, the
threat to place and nation, for example. Less than forty
years later, what was left? There were the martyrs of
Masada; but the splendour of their devotion hardly in
itself compensates for the destruction that laid Jerusalem
almost to the ground. The statesman must always seek to
preserve the ordinary man and woman from demands too
great for them to bear; an élite can make a Masada
possible, but what of lesser men? The presence of Jesus
and the Lazarus whom he allegedly brought back from
the tomb was a deeply disturbing factor, and such must
be eliminated.

Moreover, it is not only the ecclesiastical statesman
who speaks with the clear, realistic accents of Caiaphas.
The Socratic principle—the principle of following the
argument whithersoever it leads—demands that we turn
a bright light on the extent to which we indulge in
the ways in which we seek to commend the faith, a
kind of dishonest sophistry, and on our related readiness to ignore the extent to which it may be that the
ardour and skill which an individual displays in apolo-

getics frequently minister to his own self-importance. For in such corruption the apologist is too often encouraged by the churchly institution he claims to serve. Apologists are valuable; their skills are taken too often at their face value, receiving the endorsement of the institution they serve, which finds in their expertise a weapon too valuable lightly to be criticized. 'That one man should die for the people': the casualties in the decision of which I am now speaking are truth, integrity, openness of mind—but the apologist himself is among them. He is not seen as a human being with human responsibilities and human frailties; he is seen as a tool, a ζῶον ὄργανον (Aristotle's phrase for a slave, in the *Politics*), of the institution.

These last remarks may seem loosely connected with what has gone before, and indeed almost peripheral to my central theme. The young Christian in the academic world, and I have lived and worked in that world now for thirty-two years as a teacher and four years before that as a student, can easily be blind to the sort of abuse of genuine talent encouraged by ecclesiastical and quasi-ecclesiastical institutions. Men and women are taken from their proper, fundamental, professional work and the resources of their gifts mercilessly exploited in order that the Christian cause be commended. They are subject to pressures of various kinds, including (and here I speak from experience) the powerful tools of spiritual blackmail on the one side and flattery on the other. There is a characteristically Christian philistine disdain here for disinterested concern with the truth for its own sake; there is also an almost certainly deliberate encouragement of dishonesty in that university teachers receive incentives to neglect the work for which they are paid (usually out of public funds) in order to undertake the apologetic task; and there is a graver pastoral irresponsibility in that the lasting spiritual damage which is done to individuals in this way is often completely overlooked until it is too late.

Perhaps these words will suffice to show why I regard as aspects of the same kind of idolatry of the institution seen as the embodiment of an ultimate security, both the exclusiveness which expresses itself in a cruel bigotry and the blindness that refuses to query means which serve that institution's supposedly observable welfare. During the Spanish Civil War an Anglican apologist for the cause of General Franco urged the claims of his forces on the grounds that their victory would at least ensure the preservation of the external life of the Church. The situation was extreme; but the question sowed in my mind more than thirty years ago a deep scepticism concerning the value to be assigned in this present to preserving the external life of the Church, at least in forms easily recognizable as continuous with those which we know and take for granted. It is no accident that these questions are being asked radically and with greatest effect in the Church of Rome; but they are questions which we must face in our own situation and in the essentially Anglican setting of Westminster Abbey and in commemoration of Charles Gore. It is worth while that we should ask what for the life of the Anglican Communion, and especially the Church of England, is implied by the radical application of the law of *kenosis* to the evaluation of its present institutional life. Hitherto I have spoken primarily with a vivid memory of the failure of the Anglo-Catholic tradition. But I am now going to discuss the issues against a less restricted background.

At the heart of the Christian story we may see the opposition of Christ and Caiaphas: of the one who asked as a rhetorical question what shepherd, if he lost one sheep, would not leave the ninety and nine to seek it out; and the one who gave counsel that it was expedient that one man should die for the people. Whatever may survive the demythologization of the highly questionable myth of apostolic succession, empirical study of Church history reveals how often and at what depth of commitment the way of the Church has been that of Caiaphas rather than Christ. In the situation of radical unbelief with which we are confronted, we are offered, if we are prepared to be bold enough and to allow the liberating power of such ideas as *kenosis* to have their way with us, a chance which may not come again for centuries. This is the chance to lay aside the burden of the past, to begin our recovery from the disaster that, according to Father Benson, overtook the Christian Church with Constantine's conversion. But it will not be easy, and as the rest of this lecture will seek to suggest, while there will most certainly be immeasurable gains, we shall also have to be prepared to lose much that some of us cherish (myself, for the record, less than many I know), whose loss will certainly issue us into a world that we are bound to find strange, and that will be for all of us at some points uncongenial.

The word Establishment suggests inevitably, and particularly in the setting of Westminster Abbey, the constitutional position of the Church of England. Yet, although such a position is clearly incompatible with post-Constantinian realities and is widely recognized as being so, it is not of Establishment narrowly conceived that I wish primarily to speak. There are, however, two matters to which I wish to refer.

1. We hear very much today on all hands of demand for participation in decision-making processes. The term 'alienation' is freely used—in senses only loosely related

to its relatively precisely defined employment in the early writings of Karl Marx—to give expression to the sort of deprivation presently experienced by those who clamour for a greater say in the shaping of their destinies, whether in the field of national and regional government, in industry, in the world of the universities, or in the ecclesiastical world, especially in the Church of Rome. But what of the Church of England?

In the life of that Church it is a little less than eight years since the day on which Lord Fisher's announcement of his impending resignation of the primacy of all England was followed immediately by the announcement that he was to be succeeded at Canterbury by the then archbishop of York, and that the vacancy so created in the Northern Province was to be filled by the translation from Bradford of Dr Donald Coggan. So the expected presence at Canterbury of one generally regarded as an Anglo-Catholic was to be offset by the appointment to York of one equally conspicuously associated with the Evangelical tradition. No Sunday on which the *plebs sancta Dei* (the holy common people of God) assembled for worship might invoke the guidance of the Holy Spirit for those charged with the appointment of Lord Fisher's successor was allowed to intervene. The matter was judged, in the corridors of power, too important (or perhaps too insignificant) to wait on an interlude of prayer.

It would be hard to conceive a more radical denial of the most elementary right of Christian people to participate in the choice of their chief pastors, or a more contemptuous public dismissal of the claims of prayer. No one has yet suggested in so many words that the Patronage Secretary has replaced the Holy Ghost in the Church of England's understanding of the proper method for choosing its chief pastors; but its practice encourages the belief that such a substitution has taken place, or that we shall soon hear that the passages in the fourth Gospel relating to the 'Other Advocate' are to be demythologized in terms of the gift of such a functionary. But such advertised contempt for the claims of prayer inevitably and properly breeds an answering contempt for those who make themselves a party to it. This sort of bland dismissal of the assembled, common prayer of the faithful as a thing of no account is inevitably met by an answering mistrust of the men who without scruple accept appointment under such a system, and spring eagerly to its defence when it is met with challenge from the standpoint either of theology or ethics. It is my opinion (it is also, I admit, my fervent hope) that we may see radical change in this matter soon. Certainly, as a teacher concerned with Christian ethics, I regard it as my duty to do what I can to promote such a change and to point out that no Church that adheres to such methods in the choice of its chief pastors, and defends continued adherence to it on grounds of the admittedly searching consequences of substituting a more earthy, democratic procedure, has the right to speak of the ethical value of participation in other decision-making processes.

If we believe that in democracy, for all its cumbrous inconvenience on occasion, we have still the most effective method on the political plane for making power accountable to those in whose name it is exercised, we must surely be impatient to rid our Church life of the surviving remnants of structures which first took their shape in a dark age of royal absolutism.

Increasingly one sees, however, how much growth to spiritual maturity (a genuine 'coming of age') is bound up with the withdrawal of the kind of external framework which for centuries ecclesiastical authorities have taken for granted as the context of their activities. The growth of a real public contempt for accepted styles of ecclesiastical behaviour, and the dissemination of this contempt through, for instance, the satirical programmes of BBC television, is something to be positively welcomed. A study of the fourth Gospel suggests (and the lesson is continuous with the teaching of the synoptists) that Christ's subtlest foes were those who would make him king, imprisoning him so completely in the structures they would claim to erect on the foundation of their devotion that his work of being lifted up from the earth to draw all men to himself was put in jeopardy by their anxious zeal.

2. Although it is late, even desperately late in the day, one may hope that in the post-Constantinian age the Churches will be able to turn their energies again to serious engagement with the ethical problems raised by war. None would dispute that in the centuries-long story of the Churches' failure few chapters are darker than that relating to war. Where England is concerned, the passing of Establishment as we have known it would surely lead to a day in which episcopal lawn sleeves would cease to flutter in the breeze as their wearer bestowed the diocesan benediction upon the latest Polaris submarine. Here we should find sheer gain without any loss at all. Yet, at a deeper and more pervasive level, the readiness of any Church to face the implication of Father Adolfs's challenge to us all concerning the whole Constantinian era of ecclesiastical history would surely make possible a radical rethinking of the assumptions on which so much Christian debate concerning the ethical problems of war is usually conducted.

But it is not these problems so much as the ultimate sense of the concept of Establishment that I want to discuss in this lecture. Yet one word first (and here I may seem to substitute association of ideas for argument). We are told that we must choose between Establishment and the 'existence of the ghetto'. I would ask, what of the Warsaw ghetto? That was a place of suffering certainly, but one surely nearer the centre than the periphery of the world's travail. Sometimes I admit to disliking intensely the use by Christians of the term 'ghetto' in such contexts as the one I have illustrated. What indeed were, what indeed are ghettos, other than standing monuments to Christian failure across the Constantinian ages to engage with the problem of the old Israel, to seek the healing of the schism created on the first Good Friday, the first and perhaps the most horrible rent in Christ's Body. And ought we to be so sure that we should not find something in ghetto existence profoundly to be welcomed? Perhaps I stand too much here on a phrase; perhaps I am being over-sensitive linguistically; but the problem, or rather the mystery, of the old Israel should ever be with the new. And in the matter to which I have referred, we have to reckon with a supreme historical failure on the part of Christendom.

If this lecture has a unifying theme, however, it is this. What is cushioned is likely to be invalid. What encourages us to defend the security allegedly bestowed by our traditions puts our Christian understanding in peril. That understanding is imperilled also, of course, by the cult of the alleged autonomy of faith, according to which faith is creative of its own objects. Here too there is flight to a security, albeit an inward security, a withdrawal from accepting the peril and the promise of the Incarnation. It is, I repeat, not with Establishment in the narrower sense that I am concerned in this lecture, but with the cultivation of the status of invulnerability, issuing in a devotion to the structures that preserve it. This is a condition we may seek in the domain of ideas; we may also seek it on the plane of institutions, of inherited structures. The ablest contemporary apologists for the continuance of Establishment in the narrow sense have often urged the extent to which its continuance makes possible a Christian presence to the forces which direct and shape the life of our society. Their critics, on the other hand, find such presence too much a make-believe, too much a source of the illusion that we are actually exposed to the stresses and strains of the conflict between faith and unbelief, when all the time we are providing ourselves with some sort of ready-made assurance that these conflicts are resolved in a providential order that governs our comings and goings and makes all things work together for good. And it is with the critic that I myself agree.

To speak in these terms may seem a deliberate flirtation with obscurity, when what is needed is definite and clear presentation of choices to be made. But the issue of *kenosis* and Establishment is in the end an issue of spirituality. To live as a Christian in the world today is necessarily to live an exposed life; it is to be stripped of the kind of security that tradition, whether ecclesiological or institutional, easily bestows. We deceive ourselves if we suppose that we do not seek to hide ourselves away from the kind of exposure to which I am referring. To do so might quite properly be thought the besetting sin of the characteristically Anglican ethos, a cultivated avoidance of extremes. And whether we like it or not, today we do live in an extreme situation. For myself, I know that while I accept this at one level, at another I long for the sort of protection against the sharp pressure of ultimate questions that various forms of make-believe offer. I would be false to my experience if I did not include among those forms of make-believe that which is often offered as participation in Church work actively directed towards the Christian penetration of the supposed key positions in our society.

I mentioned a while back the BBC's satirical programmes. A few years ago (according to information given to me; I did not myself see the programme in question), an episode occurred which may be thought to pinpoint the lessons of this entire lecture. In a programme (not, I think, specifically satirical) a vicar was invited to speak on the significance of Christmas, only to have his words completely drowned by a clamour of eager and somewhat raucous humanist voices. Immediately the spokesman of official Christianity raised the cry of free speech, insisting on the vicar's right to be heard, etc.

Yet, profounder reflection would suggest that this 'happening' was an acted parable of the Christian situation in the contemporary world, a situation in which *omnia abeunt in silentium*. We simply have not 'got the answer' to radical unbelief (whatever the state of affairs indicated by the tendentious and misleading phrase 'having the answer' may be). 'What we cannot speak about that we must assign to silence' (Wittgenstein). Such silence is itself a kind of indirect communication, the ultimate μαρτυρία τῃ ἀληθείᾳ.

To speak in these terms is not to be guilty of irrationalism. It is to express the conviction, which at some level we all share, that in Christian belief we reach the frontiers of the intelligible, the mysterious actuality of the divine self-emptying. Certainly the writ of logic runs in the field of theology. But we cannot trace always the precise way in which it does. Thus we know (and this I have insisted in this lecture) that we must, as far as we can, eliminate self-contradiction and every other counter-intuitive element from our concepts. Yet still we may, rather we *must*, admit a final and inescapable failure to represent the manner of God's presence to the world in Christ, the quality of the transcendent decisively disclosed in him. And in this situation we do well to consider silence as a 'system of projection' of the ineffable. But it must be a silence expressed in action: not simply an unwillingly accepted aphasia. One could regard it indeed as a generalized form of the silence to which, in the great scene of Hochhuth's *Soldiers*, Bishop Bell is reduced by Churchill: a silence that bears witness to the fact that we have reached beyond argument to a place in which all that is left us is to affirm not ourselves but that to which, however haltingly, we are bound to witness.

The vicar's situation in that televised scene is a paradigm as well as a parable of the Church's acceptance of the law of *kenosis vis-à-vis* the world in which it is set. It is not to be received as an argument in favour of a cult of powerlessness or failure, recalling the well-known, deeply unhealthy cult of despair as the only *praeambula fidei*, which was fashionable in the 'forties. It is, rather, a defeat that is not a defeat, because it is eloquent of hope as well as of failure; it is suffused by a sense of promise of that which is not yet, but which is even now coming to be, which is indeed coming to be as the Church begins to realize existentially as well as theoretically the law of *kenosis*, the law of the Incarnation, by which the manner of its own fidelity is bound.

Because I am an intellectual, I am continually aware of the vulnerability of every form of apologetic, and the absence of any kind of intellectual security in believing today. Yet I know that I find these things frightening partly because I am too much the heir of a deeply false tradition of conventional apologetic, which looked for public confirmation of Christ's victory, won in the darkness and manifested to his own by the strange, unparalleled light of Easter, in the stabilities of a so-called

Christian order. There is no deeper misunderstanding of the *mysterium Christi* than that which insists, against all the evidence, in construing the resurrection as a descent from the cross, publicly and unambiguously visible to all standing around, but made the more overwhelmingly effective by a thirty-six-hour postponement. We all of us in different ways, in different situations, have to learn the extent to which we are prisoners of utterly misleading imagery concerning the nature of Christ's victory over the world and the manner of its manifestation.

So the imperative is clear to go forward, not clinging to external protection but embracing insecurity, and to go forward in hope. It is indeed on a note of hope that I would draw towards my conclusion; for I do myself regard the coming of the post-Constantinian age as occasion for the renewal of hope: this, even though I find much that frightens and distresses me because, like everyone else, I have clung and continue to cling to my own securities. (Hence indeed the detailed references to the Anglo-Catholic experience with which this lecture began.) Moreover, this hope, as we have seen, is one that ranges over a wide field, including the territory of inter-Church relations, the relation of the Church to the world in which it is set, theology and the life of the intellect, the deepest levels of spiritual awareness, etc. It is a hope big with the promise of a more inclusive, if much more costly, charity, and I would insist that for myself I see the future as likely to bring more gain than loss, provided we are bold enough and sufficiently freed from bondage to the false imagery of the past, to rise to the extent of its opportunity.

But my last word of all must be rather different. We hear much today of the supposed damage inflicted on

Christianity by Plato and the tradition springing from
him and claiming in a measure his authority. In my
judgment a great deal of such polemic is both ill-in-
formed and irrelevant. Thus it often fails to do justice to
the deepest damage that Plato's authority inflicted on
Christian tradition. I refer to the extent to which that
tradition took over Plato's flight from the tragic as an
ultimate, irreducible form of representation of the relation of the transcendent to the familiar. In the argument
of the *Republic* this criticism is a prolegomenon to its
author's attempt in the καλλιπόλις to establish a world
without ambiguity, a world from which the kind of darkness that Sophocles, for instance, had profoundly understood was expelled. For Plato it was demonstrably blas-
phemous to query the certainty of 'a happy ending'. Yet
his own dream of the καλλιπόλις was itself instinct with
that tragic quality whose irreducible presence anywhere
in the scheme of things he had so rigorously sought to
deny.

The ecclesiological fundamentalist of every school,
whether he admits it or not, finds in the actual history of
his Church something of the security the καλλιπόλις
sought to offer. He may find this security realized in the
form of the ecclesiastical structure; or he may find it
through imposing on the questionable contingencies of
his Church's history *vis-à-vis* civil society, an interpreta-
tion which makes bold use of the category of the providential. He finds in the contemplation of that history
the sort of drug which he needs to still the interrogative
temper, and the obstinate determination to ask awkward
questions and to go on asking them; he uses the study of
that history as a kind of tranquillizer whereby he can lull
himself into supposing the unknown somehow known,
the unfathomable somehow plumbed to its depths. The
ragged edges are made to disappear; the terrible reality

of human waste, to which the Churches have added so much by the ways in which they have dealt with men and women, is pushed out of sight. In God's world all must surely be for the best; how otherwise can it be his world? Yet Christ experienced dereliction, and although in faith we proclaim him raised from the dead, that resurrection did not annul the previous experience, which was its dark condition.

We are on the threshold of an age in which we are going to be able to learn these lessons anew, as we are sometimes gradually, sometimes with shocking rapidity, divested of the burdens laid on our backs by the sorry patterns of past ages. Yet we must not suppose that we shall ourselves escape the reality of the tragic in our novel situation, even if our experience makes it possible (as it has not always been in the past) for us to recognize that such reality belongs to the very stuff of the Church's existence and the Church's presence to the world.

We cannot forecast the form of the experience which awaits us; we will certainly be disappointed of many of those fears with which we anticipate the advent of the new insecurity as well as of the hopes with which we greet its coming. Loss of security will not be as frightening a thing in actuality as it is to many in prospect; exclusion from a traditionally accepted place in the ancient structure of our society is likely to prove a means of presence rather than withdrawal. Yet we will not find the καλλιπόλις, let alone the ultimate reality of the kingdom of God, in our future experience; we can only hope that because a false dream has yielded or begun to yield to a temper more deeply perceptive of the mystery of *kenosis*, we will be a little better prepared to recognize our frailty, and that it is in weakness that our strength is made perfect: in genuine weakness, not the simulated powerlessness of the spiritual poseur.

These last remarks are obscure; but prophecy is always hazardous, and we are on the threshold of an unprecedented experience. Our first duty is to free our imaginations of the kind of hesitation that comes from our archaism and our unyielding confinement within the categories and imagery of past ages. But though I believe we are about to learn deeper lessons concerning the laws of Christian existence than have been possible for centuries, these laws are still laws of Christian existence— that is, laws of existence in dependence on the one whose essence lay in his dependence on the Father. If the lessons therefore bite deep they will teach us not to seek in our future, deliverance from the tragic, but the presence of the ground that alone makes possible the endurance of its burden. I almost said the significant endurance of its burden; yet to speak in such terms would be to contradict the substance of this lecture, in that it belongs to the heart of the idea of *kenosis* that ultimate significance shall be received, not imposed.

Gore Memorial Lecture delivered in Westminster
Abbey on 5 November 1968

Theology and Tragedy

It is now some years since Professor D. Daiches Raphael published his interesting book, *The Paradox of Tragedy*, which represented one of the first serious attempts made by a British philosopher to assess the significance of tragic drama for ethical, and indeed metaphysical theory. Since then we have had a variety of books touching on related topics: for instance, Dr George Steiner's *Death of Tragedy* and Mr Raymond Williams's most recent, elusive and interesting essay, *Modern Tragedy*. To entitle an essay 'Theology and Tragedy' might be thought to invite needless trouble for oneself; to indulge to a dangerous degree the human intellectual obsession (so thoroughly castigated by Wittgenstein) of supposing that 'the meaning of a word is an object'. After all, if one confines one's regard to the Greeks, one has to recognize that between the treatments of their common theme of *Electra*, Sophocles and Euripides are in fact doing very different things. There is no gainsaying the significance for Euripides of the postponement of the murder of Clytemnestra till after that of Aegisthus, still less of his introduction into his play of the morally upright peasant, who has had the banished Electra in his keeping, and whose simple integrity contrasts both with the corruption of the court and the obsessive preoccupation with a dreadful, supposed duty of brother and sister. The element of propaganda is unmistakable; while in Sophocles' *Electra* it is altogether absent, although Dr Victor Ehrenberg in his very interesting monograph on *Sophocles and*

Pericles has argued strongly for an element of subtle political commentary in the treatment of Oedipus in the *Oedipus Tyrannus*, and of Creon in the *Antigone*. These remarks may serve to show that the title does not express a blind indifference to the multiple complexity of those works which we class together as tragedies. They are inherently complex, and various in emphasis; at best we can discern a family resemblance between them, and, in an essay like this, the author runs the risk not only of selecting examples tailor-made to his thesis but also of imposing an appearance of similarity of conception where it is at least equally important to stress differences.

'The poets knew it all already.' So Sigmund Freud; and the reader at once thinks of the remarkable fact that the theme of Oedipus' guilt is presented by Sophocles as the drama of an interrogation (it has been mentioned by historians of detective fiction as one of the first ventures in that *genre* on the stage), which becomes progressively the drama of a man's self-scrutiny, culminating in a moment, simultaneously of ἀναγνώρισις and of περιπετεία, in which he learns a truth about himself so terrible that he can no longer bear to look upon his world, and blinds himself that he may no longer see with his eyes the bearers of relationships it seems to violate the frontiers of discourse to attempt to characterize. Again in his study of *Hamlet and Oedipus*, Dr Ernest Jones, Freud's biographer, suggests that some of the complexities of the prince's behaviour become intelligible if we admit the poet's awareness of the traumatic elements in a son's relation to his mother, and to his father and his mother's lover, and indeed finds the significance of the writing of the play in the poet's biography as a 'working-out' of just such conflicts in his own life.

Yet when a philosopher recalls Freud's words, he is inclined by reason of his professional commitment, to suggest that the poets 'knew it all' only in the sense of a vague, intuitive perception which must yield place to effective articulation in terms of general concepts. True enough, neither the *Oedipus Tyrannus* nor *Hamlet* can be regarded as works of psychological theory. Yet the philosopher in the condescension towards the poets which marks his reception of Freud's words, is of course more than he may realize the heir of the ancient quarrel between the poets and the metaphysicians. If all Western philosophy is 'a series of footnotes to Plato', as Whitehead suggested, those who contribute to those footnotes may (even if they repudiate, for instance, their master's attachment to fundamental falsehood in political theory, viz. the thesis that a final solution of the problems of human order and culture can be achieved by the concentration of unfettered legislative and executive power in the hands of a carefully selected and minutely trained élite) remain, here in spite of Aristotle's sharply perceptive criticisms, blindly attached to other perilous assumptions imposed by his authority.

Plato's quarrel with the tragedians would seem to have three separable roots (I am thinking here of the *Republic*):

(1) He found in them a theology he regarded as inadmissible, viz. one that represented the gods as indifferently the authors of good and evil. One thinks here of the concluding passages of Sophocles' *Trachiniae*, laying responsibility for the terrible events of that play, by turns fantastic, horrifying, shocking, humanly outrageous, and expressive of a kind of religious devotion (I refer to the manner of Heracles' cremation) fairly and squarely on the shoulders of heaven. This, it is implied, is the way the world is; thus the hero, who has laid all Hellas in his debt by the range and extent of his labours, after he first

degenerates into a drunkard, who will make war upon a city to recompense an insult or to gratify a lust, comes to his end; thus his wife, Deianira, a woman caught up in a monstrous world of demi-gods, patient, in a genuine way capable of more than a measure of compassion in her treatment of Iole (commentators have contrasted it with Clytemnestra's attitude to Cassandra), eager to regain her husband's love, and guilty, in her pursuit of that end, of nothing worse than folly in her use of the shirt of Nessus, encompasses both the death of her husband and her own death, unforgiven to the last by the hero to whom she had remained loyal; so it is that Iole, the object of Heracles' desire, becomes the wife of Hyllus, his son. This is the way things are; we can represent these events; we can even, in the deeply tragic figure of Deianira, suggest the extent to which men and women are trapped less by their weakness than by what is accounted virtue in them. (In Deianira's case, it is her tenderness which betrays her. A more formidable woman would have pursued a grimmer stratagem with a less destructive result.) This theology Plato repudiates, stating quite dogmatically that the gods are the authors only of that which is good; the origin of evil remains opaque; but we cannot attribute it to heaven. There is, of course, later in the *Republic* with the development of the notion of τὸ μὴ ὀν, the ontological correlate of ἀγνωσία, more than a suggestion of the later, developed, ontological characterization of evil as 'not-being', in the sense of privation: (a view of which I will only here say that it has only to be stated clearly, and worked out in terms of concrete examples, to be shown to be totally inadequate as an analysis either of moral or of physical evil. Of this doctrine, I would echo words often used by the late Professor H. A. Prichard: 'Whatever is true, that can't be!'). But in Book II, when establishing canons of theological censorship, and developing, in the context thereof, criteria of the theoretically admissible in theology, Plato contents himself with insisting that even as we know *a priori* that the concept of divine metamorphosis is internally self-contradictory, so we know *a priori* that the theologumena with which the *Trachiniae* ends are likewise inadmissible. Even as the notion of the construction of the regular heptagon is mathematically impossible (I use an example employed in other connections by Wittgenstein), so the notion of a god who is the author of the evils that overtook Heracles and Deianira is the notion of an *Unding*.

(2) Closely connected with the above is the falsehood which Plato discerned, or thought that he discerned, in the suggestion that the virtuous man or woman could be overtaken by catastrophe, which touched the very substance of his or her life, leaving him or her, it may be, the helpless prey of evil men or of natural adversity, or else disintegrated within and destroyed. Plato's preoccupation in his ethical writings with the consequences in terms of reward of well-doing must be seen in this context. If he writes sometimes almost as a utilitarian, for whom personal morality may be recommended on prudential grounds, and at others (for instance in his portrait of the tyrant in Book IX of the *Republic*) as one who would present virtue as its own reward by a revelation of successful evil-doing as its own punishment, he does so because he is deeply at war with the suggestion, undoubtedly present in some tragedies, that there is evidence for the ontological irrelevance of moral goodness in the manifest discrepancy between, for example, gentleness (in Deianira), or fidelity to justice and truth (in Sophocles' portrayal of Electra), and the outward rewards and inward recompense achieved through the exercise of these virtues by those who have thus schooled themselves in them.

(3) Finally, attention to tragedy encouraged the attitude of the φιλοθεάμων, and substituted for the movement
from the many to the one (as fundamental to Plato's map
of the *itinerarium mentis ad Bonum* as to his ontology,
and as Aristotle saw, one of the most damaging, un-
criticized assumptions of his thought) the review of a
whole series of examples of human experience. Agamem-
non and Clytemnestra, Orestes, Pylades, Electra, Chryso-
themis, Ajax, Medea, Hecuba, Andromache, Priam,
Heracles, Prometheus—we pass them in review; we look
at their predicament, now from one perspective, now
from another. We enlarge our sympathies maybe; but
this we do at the cost of forgetting that there is a pearl of
great price to be won if we concentrate our energies and
our attention upon the one that stands over against the
many, from which the many derive, and which in its
transcendent dignity will establish our flickering resolve
by revealing the way of life of the saint as the surest in-
timation of the ultimate.

Even those who disregard Plato's theory of forms, except as a splendid example of revisionary metaphysics,
criticized and even discarded by its own author when in
the *Parmenides* he brought out the sheerly unintelligible
uses to which he had bent the notions of παρουσία,
μεθέξις and μιμήσις in its exposition, and in the *Sophist*
and *Theaetetus* turned instead to fundamental questions
in the philosophy of logic—even they unconsciously adhere to his relegation of tragedy to a very secondary rôle
in the enlargement of our understanding of the world
around us. At best it may provide us with exemplary
material; but serious exposition of the nature of what is
will be left to more general, and more subtly organized
statement. What is sometimes forgotten, however, is the
extent to which Plato might in fact have found, in the

central theme of the *Republic*, the subject presented un-
forgettably in the long, complementary requests made of
Socrates by Glaucon and Adeimantus—two young men
revealing, in the style of their scepticism, the sort of
urgent restlessness *vis-à-vis* the 'Idea of the Good' of which
he speaks in Book VI—the stuff of tragedy. The passage in
which the theme of the *Republic* is set is one of the great
passages of moral philosophy; hardly anywhere else is the
issue of the ontological import of moral excellence more
clearly or more unflinchingly presented. Its architecture
is admirable, and the manner in which the two young
men complement each other is perfectly designed to the
purpose of the whole. Thus Adeimantus buttresses the
theoretical queries of Glaucon with recollection of what
he has gleaned in the way of moral education, not from
the self-conscious arguments of a Thrasymachus or a
Callicles, but from the scale of priorities he has discerned
to operate in the casual appraisals he has heard passed on
the lives of those around him. But the central opposition
is that of the perfectly just and the perfectly unjust man,
with the portrait of the latter filled in by the detail of the
myth of Gyges, reminding the reader that supreme effec-
tiveness in human life is only achieved when disregard of
the sanctions of traditional morality is made possible by
the acquisition, whether by effort, by inheritance, by
good fortune, by opportunity or by a mixture of all alike,
of unchallengeable predominance on the plane of power.
Which of the two has the root of the human matter in
him—the historical Socrates, or Pericles? The latter is
represented by Thucydides as a supreme political realist,
admitting the element of tyranny in the Athenian ἀρχή
but justifying it by reference to the enormous human
superiority of the Athenian system over against the Spar-
tan, ready to use without hesitation the resources put at
her disposal by Athens's allies in the Delian confederacy,

and continuing to do so for purposes which he believed at once Athenian and, in a measure, universal, even if the peace of Callias had terminated open hostilities with Persia and thus apparently brought to an end the *raison d'être* of the confederacy. And if we are honest, we must admit that Pericles had a case against the historical Socrates, as Plato saw him, against the man whose image we catch in *Euthyphro, Apology, Critio, Phaedo,* and in whose school Alcibiades was partly formed, whose scrupulosity inhibited action, and the inconclusiveness of whose positive doctrine encouraged a scepticism more ultimately corrosive than any suggested by the most destructive sophistic teaching. Further, we must remember, in spite of Plato, that we can see a sample of the moral insight the Sophists enabled men to gain, in, for instance, the treatment by Euripides of the vengeance of Electra and Orestes to which we have already referred.

Thus what for Plato is the *point de départ* of an essay in revisionary metaphysics is also the stuff of which tragedy is made. To say this is not to subscribe to an Hegelian conception of tragic conflict as the conflict of two opposing systems of right. In his judgment on the *Antigone,* Hegel is wrong inasmuch as Antigone, for all the obsessive quality of her preoccupation with Polyneices and the Amazonian temper she displays towards Ismene, is a nobler human being, serving a higher cause than Creon, identifying, as he does, the security of the πόλις with his own personal dignity. Had Plato used as his 'system of projection', for engaging with the problems presented by Glaucon and Adeimantus, tragic drama, he would not of course have been Plato; he might incidentally have avoided some of his most disastrous mistakes in political theory; but we do not see the theory of forms as an essay in revisionary metaphysics aright unless we see that it is offered in part as an alternative way of dealing with one of the issues that, across the centuries, those who have written tragedies have sought to explore.

So Shakespeare in *Julius Caesar* (the only work in the English language on the subject of political obligation that engages with the problems facing the German conspirators against Hitler in July 1944, as Mr R. H. S. Crossman rightly pointed out) reveals Brutus betrayed into make-believe, a kind of sad self-deception concerning the bloody details of the purpose to which he has lent himself, and then by his continuing scruple, into the sort of *fainéantise* that dooms his enterprise to disaster (I am thinking of his insistence that Antony be spared), but still remaining a man of nobler stuff than the other figures in the play. No one can doubt this who sets over against each other Brutus' scrupulosity, and the quick, resolute ruthlessness of the Triumvirs (including the very young Octavius) in the short scene of the proscription. The evil that Caesar did lives after him: 'O, Julius Caesar, thou art mighty yet.' Brutus is the victim of Caesar's ambition as well as of his own folly and unwillingness to face to the full the moral issues of assassination, preferring to see in a murder a ritual act whereby the city is purified, as it were, by a 'holy and unbloody sacrifice'. Yet this unwillingness is born of his nobility, of the scrupulosity which makes him so ill-adjusted to the more effective Cassius, and which reveals him as a human being of better stuff than the Triumvirs, in whose cold and detached listing of their victims the evil that Caesar did is revealed as triumphantly alive.

But what have these considerations to do with theology? We are often told (this is Professor Raphael's view, although he admits a partial exception in the Jansenist Racine) that there is no place for tragedy in the Judaeo-Christian world-view. But is this in fact true of the Gospels as we have them? If we recall the 'open-textured

quality' (the *Porosität*) of the concept of tragedy, can we
be quite sure that it does not apply in full measure,
mutatis omnibus mutandis, to the Christian story, especially, for instance, if we allow our imaginations to include, within the compass of that story, such terrible
sequelae as the intrusion of a theologically founded anti-
Semitism into the public prayer and private imaginations
of generations of Christians, even conceivably into the
text of the New Testament itself, in, for instance, the
Gospel according to St Matthew and the Acts of the
Apostles, and even the Gospel according to St John?
Whatever may be true of Judaism, there is a sense in
which Christianity demands to be presented as the
tragedy of Jesus, of the one who, for intentions that the
believer must judge of supreme significance, abdicated
any responsibility that his influence might have con-
ferred on him to arrest the movement of his people towards the final catastrophe of A.D. 70. The Christian believes that in Christ's passion he finds at once the judgment and the redemption of the world; it is a desperately
human occasion fraught not with a great, but with an
ultimate, significance. But it is also failure; and that not
in the language of devotion, but in that of literal fact. It
is in the figure of Judas Iscariot that the failure of Jesus is
focussed, and the tragic quality of his mission becomes
plain, 'Good were it for this man if he had not been
born.' Yet through his agency the Son of Man goes his
appointed way, and of his own choice; for in a few hours'
time, he will say: 'Thy will, not mine, be done.' There is
no solution here of the problem of the moral evil; there is
nothing moreover which the Easter faith somehow ob-
literates. For it is to his own, and not to the world, that
the risen Christ shows himself; and even those who accept
as factual the record of the empty tomb admit that in
itself that emptiness is no more than a sign pointing.

We need perhaps to explore with very great care the sense in which the term 'tragic' may significantly be predicated of the Gospel records. Such an exploration may throw more light than we expect on the question of the 'system of projection' appropriate to the Christian reality; but it is also bound to raise, within the context of Christian theology, questions analogous to those which Plato regarded as so serious that he tried to discredit altogether the claim of tragic drama to represent the notion of what is—and that on theological grounds!

Religious Studies, 1967

Authority and Freedom in the Church

No one concerned with questions of religious truth today can long escape the problem of freedom and authority. The issue has recently been pinpointed by the decision of the Roman Catholic theologian, Charles Davis, to leave his Church, both because he rejects certain doctrines and because he repudiates the method by which his Church as an institution constrains its members, both clerical and lay, not only to adhere to formally defined dogmas, but to submit to the deliverances of its ordinary *magisterium* and even the day-to-day policies and decisions of its executive authority. Charles Davis's action expressed not only an intellectual but also a moral revolt. He was making a costly protest against an institution which in its workings seemed to set obstacles in the way of Christian living rather than help to promote its growth.

If we begin by distinguishing these two elements in Davis's protest, we soon see that the moral aspect of his protest is also of profound theological significance, for he is raising the theological problem of the Church as an institution; of the manner in which, as an institution, it exercises authority over its members. By implication he is raising the whole theological question of the forms in which the Church's allegedly apostolic mission is carried on.

Davis's action is admittedly a response to the extreme situation which he has encountered in the most authoritarian of all the Churches, the Church of Rome. Inevitably it seems a comment on a whole number of episodes, some publicly known and many more not, in the recent history of that Church. For instance, one thinks of the intellectual damage unquestionably done to the visionary Teilhard de Chardin by the decision to inhibit publication of his writings during his lifetime, and to prevent him from taking up the kind of academic post in France that would have made it possible for him to submit his ideas to the kind of criticism which they badly needed. The history of his development reveals how he was driven in upon himself, and in consequence was encouraged by isolation to adopt eccentric and un-balanced attitudes. (To say this, of course, is not to deny his genius; it is only to remind ourselves of his tragedy.)

But Davis's action is something of wider significance; it has lessons to teach men who have not been exposed to the sorts of pressure that clearly he has known, but who are none the less dimly aware that they must face the theological and ethical problems raised by Churches as institutions.

My own experience is Anglican; and it is almost a commonplace to remark that in practice the Anglican Communion, and especially the Church of England, is the least authoritarian of the Churches. Yet the ecclesi-astical temper encourages its leaders, encourages also those who undertake the spiritual direction of its mem-bers, to allow the end to justify the means. 'It is ex-pedient that one man should die for the people': in these words of Caiaphas we catch an indelible impression of the attitude of mind of the responsible ecclesiastic. They express the major premise of a great many practical syllogisms whose conclusion is always the same; that the individual shall be broken, or that his or her claims shall be disregarded.

I am mainly concerned with the problem of intel-lectual freedom, with the question of the attitude of

authority towards searching inquiry touching the very
foundations of faith, with the posture that the inquirer
himself may properly adopt in face of that authority; but
I want to set the question in the context of a theological,
even a Christological, exploration of the nature of
humility, the humility in particular demanded of those
who exercise authority in the Church of Christ. To
approach the matter in this way, however, reveals that
the principles with which we are concerned have a wider
relevance and require application in many other connections, if the ministry of the Church is to reflect the
image of the servant-God.

'To follow the argument withersoever it leads.' This
Socratic injunction is supposedly a categorical imperative
for anyone who would philosophize, however much he
may fail in practice to fulfil its precepts. But can anyone
who is in some sense committed to Christian faith allow
himself, or be allowed by authority, a comparable freedom? The question which I have heard most searchingly
put—did not the Church spoil so-and-so as a philosopher?—is one that can have a number of senses. For
instance, it may refer to a deflection of intellectual
energies imposed by external authority; but it may also
advertise a more subtle, interior willingness to turn aside
from the queries that reach to the very foundations. This
is a turning aside which ecclesiastical authority encourages by the use not only of psychological deterrents but
also of more insidious incentives.

One may, however, use the language of this question—
did not the Church spoil so-and-so as a philosopher?—to
ask whether it is *logically* possible for a man to acknowledge a divine self-disclosure, and an ultimately significant divine action in a particular set of historical events,
and remain open at all levels to expanding intellectual
horizons and to the necessity of enlarging, deepening,

and revising his moral perceptions. Even if one allows that an affirmative answer to this question about openness is *logically* possible, one has still to concede the extent to which the pressures of ecclesiastical authority and institutional convention combine to sap the interrogative, unaccommodating temper of the inquirer and substitute for his restless eagerness the more submissive and conformist temper of the apologist.

Such submission is frequently counselled in the name of humility, of humility at once towards God and towards one's fellows: it is certainly, as we shall see, near to the heart of the Christian revelation that humility is a fundamental attribute of the divine as disclosed in Christ, and therefore, inasmuch as Christ is consubstantial with the Father who sent him and no mere simulacrum of the one whom he characterizes as greater than himself, an attribute of the divine as it is in itself. But humility is more often than not presented as a kind of submissive obedience to the Church's traditions, to her institutional and organizational development, irrespective of the historical and social factors which may have shaped it, and the built-in consequences of the past decisions of her leaders.

Much less is said of the extent to which those who exercise such authority must display humility in their turn; much less too of the extent to which the styles of triumphalism in, say, the Roman Catholic Church, or (again I speak as an Anglican) the elaborate ceremonial masquerade of Establishment distort not only the manner but the substance of an apostolic presence to the world.

In the last analysis it is with the manner of such presence that we are concerned; with the manner, too, of the Church's witness to the truth. This emerged very clearly in the affair of the French worker-priests in the early 'fifties. It was not simply the deep political involve-

ment of many individuals that prompted brutal intervention by Rome; it was the worker-priests' obvious pre-
ference for a method of getting alongside people where
they are to one suggesting the declaration of a truth delivered from on high which offended authority.

The apostle is able to teach only so far as he is also
learning; learning all the time. This is the way of presence. The ecclesiastic fears it because it robs him of the
security which he finds for his own status and mission, as
long as he can continue to address both his inferiors and
his prospective converts as it were *de haut en bas*, as a
Christ descended from the pinnacle of the temple, silenc-
ing questions by a manifestation of power, but by that
action withdrawing himself from the common way of
men and women, from both the constant and the tran-
sient conditions of their lives.

You may well ask at this point whether this kind of
approach does not argue for a complete abrogation of
authority in matters of religious belief, or at least suggest
that those in whom such authority is vested be required
to abdicate their proper responsibilities. It may indeed be
said that the temper of the approach is more that of John
Stuart Mill's *Essay on Liberty* than, let us say, that of
Paul's Second Letter to the Corinthians. We must concede a responsibility to ecclesiastical authority for safe-
guarding what is sometimes called, in a rather misleading
phrase, the 'deposit of faith'; but such authority must also
acknowledge the cutting edge of the question: *quis cus-
todiet ipsos custodes?*—who will guard the guardians?
What is at issue is not the need of mitigating the impact
of irresponsible and random speculation and experiment,
but the manner in which such direction is imposed, and
also the limitations of its scope.

This, I argue, is a theological question. Of course, 'we
have this treasure in earthen vessels'; and these earthen

vessels include historical institutions. But those who help to maintain and operate them must always remember just how much these institutions are the products less of divine providence than of the grisly complexities and accidents of human history. To serve them, no doubt, is a psychologically satisfying rôle for those called to exercise office and administration in them; it may indeed become so satisfying a rôle that it inhibits all power to criticize, all power to recognize the need for radical renewal, even for that kind of transformation which can only be described in terms of death and resurrection.

There is a passage towards the end of Whitehead's *Process and Reality* which is very illuminating here:

'When the Western world accepted Christianity, Caesar conquered; and the received text of Christian theology was edited by his lawyers. The code of Justinian and the theology of Justinian are two volumes expressing one movement of the human spirit. The brief Galilean vision of humility flickered through the ages, uncertainly. In the official formulation of the religion it has assumed the trivial form of the mere attribution to the Jews that they cherished a misconception about their Messiah. But the deeper idolatry, of the fashioning of God in the image of the Egyptian, Persian and Roman imperial rulers, was retained. The Church gave unto God the attributes which belonged exclusively to Caesar.'

One can hardly overpraise the insight of this passage, especially the unerring diagnostic precision with which it shows how Christendom has succeeded across the ages in ignoring the overwhelming Christological implications of such a saying as 'I am amongst you as he that serves', by externalizing its catastrophic theological import in terms of an alleged Jewish refusal to see how (or that) Jesus fulfilled the messianic rôle.

Whitehead is inaccurate in his choice of the word 'Galilean' to convey the heart of the matter on which he has laid his finger; what he so characterizes by a geographical expression is as much of Jerusalem, synagogue, temple-courts, upper room, praetorium and place of execution as it is of lakeside, hillside, Capernaum, Tiberias; but he is utterly right to fasten on the extent to which the fusion of the faith of the Incarnation with a cultural whole, including Hebraic, Greek and Roman elements, has issued in a disastrous subordination of the mysteries of the self-revealing, the self-giving, the serving God, to a highly wrought complex of ideas ultimately hardly compatible with what has been disclosed.

Rightly, Whitehead fastens first on the Roman ingredient, the extrapolation of the concept of executive imperial *gubernaculum,* to convey the idea of a supremely authoritative providence, delegating his powers to those whom he has bidden in his stead to guide and rule his people. This spirit is not only manifested in the Church of Rome; we see it wherever institutional Christianity, when called to answer the question of the nature of its authority, does so in terms of direction in accordance with laws more or less clearly formulated, or (here I am thinking of the Church of England as by law established) by reference to a position constitutionally assured.

There is no doubt in my mind that the Anglican appeal to the alleged position of the Church of England in the life of this country as an unalterable constant does often play a disastrous rôle in stifling the spread of intellectually and ecclesiologically radical ideas. The appeal rests, of course, on a falsification of the facts of history; one has only to remember the seventeenth century to see this. But, worse, it encourages the kind of intellectually frivolous pragmatism that today we simply cannot afford, and it also ministers to a most offensive kind of spiritual pride.

If we are to pursue more than a make-believe theological radicalism, we must find in what Whitehead calls the 'brief Galilean vision of humility' the sources of a deep renewal of Christological, indeed of *essential* Trinitarian understanding. But this renewal will come only if we set our theological imaginations in a hard light, and acknowledge the corrupting effects of history upon them, being ready to criticize sharply and to resist any tendency to represent the ways of God with men in terms of a particular cultural and political stabilization of human forces. Whether our ecclesiastical leaders recognize it or not, we confront the unlimited opportunities, as well as perils, of a post-Constantinian age.

There is something almost pathetic (if it were not also so coldly cruel in its manifestations) about the ways in which ecclesiastical authority seeks to retain the styles of a past age. In the Church of Rome we have had since the Modernist movement repeated instances of authority's seeking to coerce or break the individual, without any sense of that authority being itself a kind of partner to a dialogue which must, I will not say go on, but rather be set in motion to further the cause of apostolic presence in the world. I will mention two recent examples within the Church of England. In 1966 we saw prelatical authority intervene to apparently destructive effect in the affairs of the Sheffield Industrial Mission, while blandly refusing any explanation for an action that many still regard as scandalous. Justice may have been done: it certainly does not seem to have been done. And many would say the same over the appointment to the deanery of Guildford in 1961.

It would be unfair, in this general context, not to notice the way in which some who are called radical in parts of their theology—in their approach to the New Testament, for instance—combine a nearly complete scepticism concerning the historical life of Jesus of Nazareth with what I can only call an ecclesiological fundamentalism. By an 'ecclesiological fundamentalism' I mean a readiness to accept the historical experience of the Church as self-justifying. Such men are happy to find that any external norm by which its development may be judged is unattainable.

It is easy to see how such a theology (which it is ironic to recall was that of the more extreme Catholic Modernists) issues in an admiring apologetic for actual ecclesiastical institutions. At bottom, of course, it is anti-intellectual; it is also profoundly conservative, in the end identifying what is with what ought to be, and therefore of course it has its peculiar appeal for Anglicans. All the roughness, untidiness, the perplexed, even tormented, self-interrogation that belongs to Christian belief in this century are subtly blurred, softened, and made to vanish away. We are a long way from the deep spiritual perception of those Spanish Catholics, mentioned by the late Albert Camus in his study of revolt in human life, whose faith in the sacraments remained undimmed, while they refused in prison to receive them in protest against their Church's endorsement of the methods and styles of the regime which supposedly had saved and preserved its external life. Their action is almost self-contradictory; but it is profoundly, even passionately, Christian in inspiration.

It may seem that in what I have been saying I have moved a long way from the simpler, less harrowing issues of intellectual freedom. But the enormities of which the intellectual is made aware belong to the same family. He is asked to prostitute his gifts in the cause, not of inquiry, but of the service and defence of an institution, some of whose historically acquired habits must surely repel him. He must not, of course, ask for power without responsibility; but he is right to see in his situation a parable of the need of all the Churches to renew in this day and age their understanding of the manner of their apostolic presence to the world. And that renewal demands a contemporary recovery of the sense and inwardness of Christ's own apostolate. If we are told that the state of the evidence makes such recovery impossible, and that we are left with the institution or nothing, then some of us, if we are honest, will say that we must content ourselves with that nothing and admit that faith, always precarious, is no longer a way that we can follow.

To say these things openly is not to court the easy rewards of a masquerade boldness, but rather to suggest that authority in the present is only effectively exercised in a setting of acknowledged doubt—a doubt to which it may be we are commanded by the imperative of faith itself.

BBC Third Programme, March 1967

Intercommunion: a Comment

The 'Open Letter' to which reference is made in the following article, was presented to the archbishops of Canterbury and York in the autumn of 1961, and released to the press on November 2nd of that year. It was signed by a number of Anglicans, mainly, though not exclusively, concerned with the teaching of theology and cognate subjects, and urged the necessity of an immediate readiness on the part of the Anglican Communion to acknowledge the authenticity of the sacramental ministry of those Churches, which had rejected the historic episcopate, and whose ministers had in consequence, not received episcopal ordination. This attitude should express itself in a readiness on the part of Anglicans (in appropriate circumstances) to avail themselves of such sacramental ministrations and to admit, without let or hindrance to Communion at Anglican altars all persons who (although not episcopally confirmed) were recognized as full members of their own Churches, and who desire to receive the holy sacrament at an Anglican celebration of the Eucharist.

In short, the letter advocated mutual acceptance here and now of their sacramental ministries of Churches formally each separated one from another. It pressed the importance of such a step on Anglicans in particular, as, in their recent history, they had become popularly identified with a rigorously exclusive attitude, over the admission to Communion of those not confirmed by a bishop, and over the receiving of the sacrament of the Lord's Body and Blood from the hands of a minister who had not received episcopal ordination. It was thought that for Anglicans to make such gestures at once of welcome and of acceptance in the situation of 1961 might help to release resources of mutual understanding, and indeed of charity, desperately needed if the hopes of healing the rents in Christ's Body were not to perish from long disappointment.

As one who had been more actively identified with the Anglo-Catholic tradition than any of the other signatories of the 'Open Letter', I hesitated a great deal longer than they did before signing. Yet in the end I became convinced that their cause was that not only of charity but of truth, and I added my signature almost at the last moment! Some weeks later I wrote the following article to clear my own mind, and to defend my action to those who had been surprised and even shocked by it. This article was published in *Theology* for February 1962 and as its argument coheres with that of the other pieces in this volume it is included with them.   *December 1968*

The recent publication of an 'Open Letter' to the archbishops of Canterbury and York on the subject of intercommunion was a controversial act. Although the signatories could plead that their intention was to urge a reconsideration of present policies and attitudes rather than to provoke controversy, their action was inevitably controversial in consequence. The criticisms immediately called forth have been of two kinds. To some the letter has seemed an intolerable intrusion on the part of so-called theologians into matters which must inevitably seem quite different and much more difficult when viewed from the standpoint of the parish priest; moreover the manner of the letter's publication was thought by many of these critics to display a wanton disregard of the 'proper channels' for raising issues of this kind, viz. the Convocations. To others, however, the letter has seemed the work of irresponsible and impatient men, swayed by their hearts rather than by their heads, deceiving themselves into believing that they could pursue charity at the expense of truth.

Thus the letter has been criticized both as the expression of academic, theological arrogance, and as the work of impatient men, carried away by the force of overwhelming emotion. If therefore its publication is to be justified, it must be shown as the action of men who were both intellectually aware of what they were doing, and also conscious of the limitations both of their insight and of their viewpoint. In this short article the present writer is speaking only for himself; but he is tolerably sure that for those who designed the letter, and for those who for various reasons found themselves compelled to sign it, its preparation and publication represented only a stage in a continuing action. That action, moreover, is one which must be continued, not in the preparation of manifestos and demonstrations, but in deep personal engagement with the issues raised. For the issues are ones which come up most acutely at the level of ordinary human life in the world. Thus, critics of the letter, who urge theologians and academics to recall how artificial and privileged their situation is, are saying something very important. It is hard not to be irritated by those who continually refer to the traumatic experience someone has undergone at a 'youth conference' somewhere or other. Few people spend more than a very limited period of their lives at youth conferences, and the experience gained at such gatherings is artificial and restricted, although no doubt valuable. Where these islands are concerned (and the Scottish situation is very different from the English), these issues have got to be *schematized* (if a philosopher of religion may borrow Kant's language) in terms of the sorts of situation which arise in quite ordinary towns and villages.

But what are the issues, and what of the manner in which they are to be faced? Look at the term—*intercommunion*. We are all of us familiar with the kind of controversial positions which men assume as soon as they hear the word. We have all of us assumed them in our time. A. says, 'Before all else we must remember that the Lord's Table is the Lord's, not ours'; B. replies, 'Intercommunion is the goal of our effort to be brought to unity in the truth; it cannot be the means.' And then, as an apologetic rider, B. reminds his antagonist that in England the Free Churches which have long practised intercommunion are not apparently all that nearer to organic unity. Is it not worth inquiring whether this kind of argument, valuable no doubt in its time, is not now become sterile through much repetition, even as discussion of related questions of ministry has become sterile through *exclusive* concentration on such notions as validity? Thus, should we not quite properly ask much more closely about those persons whose joining together in Holy Communion is under discussion, and what it is that they are being invited to do?

No one whose experience is confined to Western Europe and largely to these islands can fail, if he is honest, to be impressed by the demand that he consider objectively the situation of the Christian minorities in Asia, in India, in the emergent African nations, and that he make the effort to see with their eyes, and to feel with their hearts, the burdens we lay upon them by bidding them accept the consequences of our dark and terrible religious history as a necessary constituent of the 'good news' of Christ. We all pay lip-service to the importance of a sense of historical relativity; we need to practise that awareness in our lives, and not dignify a tragi-comic spiritual imperialism with the name of fidelity to the traditions which we have received. Yet the same principles, which bid us concede a genuine autonomy to the so-called 'younger Churches' and accept its fruits, must guide us in our more intimate relations here at home.

'We have all sinned and come short of the glory of God.' In concrete terms, in the sphere of inter-Church relations, that means that we are all of us the spiritual heirs of men and women who were ready to persecute or to acquiesce in persecution. It is impossible here to underestimate the importance of the issues raised by Professor C. H. Dodd in his 'open letter' on 'non-theological factors' promoting disunity, which was written as part of the preparatory material for the Lund Conference on Faith and Order in 1952. By reminding, e.g. the English, Scottish and Irish delegates of the wrongs to which their ancestors had been severally parties in the seventeenth century, he brought discussion down to earth. 'The blood of the martyrs is the seed of the Church.' Yet if the martyrs of the sixteenth and seventeenth centuries were 'united in the strife that divided them', from the manner in which their witness was exacted from them there sprang, not simply that which belongs in some sense to the Church of Christ, but traditions of life and culture estranged in all sorts of ways one from another. Professor Dodd spoke of the factors to which he called attention as 'non-theological'; and there, in my submission, he was wrong in paying lip-service to a tradition which artificially restricts the reference of the term 'theological'. What he advertised touches the substance of Christian life as it is received and lived, and the deep analysis of its origin, fruit and consequence belongs, if anything, to theology.

But what has this to do with 'intercommunion'? A great deal, inasmuch as we are now turning our attention towards the communicants who are actual men and women, sustained and illuminated, irritated and sometimes infuriated by particular traditions of Christian life and thought. Where the sacrament of the Lord's Supper is concerned, we must not neglect the actualities of concrete traditions and received (and deeply cherished) insights. Here again we seek a way through the sterility of debate between those who pretend a (non-existent) general agreement in eucharistic doctrine, and those who insist that there can be no intercommunion between those who understand the rite as differently as an Anglo-Catholic and a Zwinglian. 'It is better to give than to receive.' How wise the man who, commenting on this text, remarked that he was relieved, because to give was usually much easier than to receive! 'Giving and receiving'—I want to suggest most seriously that we (and here I address Anglicans) approach the difficult question of intercommunion by way of a consideration of what is involved in concrete terms in giving and receiving. We must not pretend to a unity of understanding which we have not attained. If we do that, we deceive ourselves; and although we may profess and call ourselves liberals, we know that we are guilty of a kind of make-believe, and therefore we are at war with ourselves. Let us admit that a tendency to hold on to what we have inherited or made our own is a powerful factor in our behaviour; let us admit that such fidelity is a protection against the kind of indifferentism which may often seek to masquerade as open-mindedness or even courage; let us admit, moreover, that such receptivity on our part can be a parable of a true response to God's grace (although it can also be something very different). But having said this, let us go on to ask to learn to receive from other traditions, at as deep a level as we can, that is at the level of sacramental communion.

In fact, of course, we Anglicans in England have already received, in other ways, very much from those from whom we are separated, whose ancestors, in fact, we persecuted; and this not only in the relatively restricted spheres of religion and theology in the conventional sense, but in much that pertains most intimately to the health of our national life, for which as members of an established Church, we are supposed to have a special responsibility. Few of us in our serious moments would dare claim that the Christian tradition of England could dispense as easily with the strength of the 'nonconformist conscience' as it could for instance with the highly questionable, class-distorted religion of the largely Anglican so-called 'public schools'.

To write in these terms is not to be guilty of theological irresponsibility. Rather it may be justifiably suggested that the writer is laying upon ordinary men and women the burden of a very hard task. But the healing of our unhappy divisions must surely be just such a work. It is indeed this to which those who counsel patience are bearing witness. Only, like others in other matters, they are inclined to take the sheer difficulty, the costliness of the enterprise, as an argument that we should do nothing at all but wait. It is significant that in the almost obsessive preoccupation with episcopacy which characterizes so much ecumenical discussion today, little or no time seems to be left for a grave meditation of the inwardness of Christ's words concerning the mission of the Holy Ghost—'I have many things to say unto you; but ye cannot bear them now. Howbeit when he, the Spirit of Truth is come,' etc. Of course, this is but one manifestation of a pervasive distortion of theological activity, and dissipation of theological energy, to which we must return in the concluding section of this article; but it is a manifestation of peculiarly poignant import for the article's first preoccupation.

For it is indeed to the working within us of the Holy Spirit that we all of us must turn, if we are to make the effort to overcome our divisions. It must be said without qualification that if a blindness towards what Professor Dodd indicated by the term 'non-theological factors' characterizes the traditionally devout, it is also displayed continually in the behaviour of the good 'conference men and women' of the ecumenical movement. The present writer has been spared the kind of traumatic experience that many claim to have had at youth conferences; but he recalls having had on two occasions to protest vehemently when invited to take part in highly select consultations on Anglican- (Scottish) Presbyterian relations to be held in the depths of Sussex! Simple economic facts would ensure that such meetings could only be utterly unrepresentative and their discussions correspondingly trivial. It would be hard to estimate too highly the damage done to serious efforts to grow into unity by this sort of unself-critical ecumenical sectarianism. The critics of the 'Open Letter' are abundantly justified in their insistence that, where England is concerned, the issues must be seen in terms of their presence in the concrete life of the parishes. Where they are wrong is in their refusal to accept as inescapable spiritual facts the abundant life of Christian traditions other than their own. In the artificial, enclosed life of Anglo-Catholic Oxford, the present writer, although frequently at that time in demand as a speaker at ecumenical gatherings, could remain insulated from the inward effect of Christian division. In Scotland this was impossible. There, as one whose attachment to the minority Anglicanism of that land was and is incomparably deeper than ever it could be or can be to the institutional reality of the C. of E., the pressure could only be felt much more severely; and that not because of the majesty of the Church of Scotland, a national Church today in a sense in which the Church of England is not, but rather because of that Church's readiness, *on the whole*, to accept and to try to learn. To write in these terms must not be accounted disloyal. The heart and centre of this article, where inter-Church relations are concerned, lies in its serious attempt to raise the problem of giving and receiving, and to raise the further question of the way in which that problem must be faced in terms of actual, local worshipping Christian Churches.

Where the theology of the Eucharist is concerned, what is here advocated as an approach to intercommunion clearly implies an attitude at first sight paradoxical. No effort must be made to slur over the realities of disagreement, or the depths and seriousness of estrangement in respect of eucharistic understanding. We must all of us, with a new profundity and a new simplicity, learn at once to reverence what we have received, and by going to the traditions of others to learn of them, to set what we cherish under the judgment of Christ. I almost said—'of justification by faith'. But I suspect that to use such a phrase (however surely understood) might for some at least conceal rather than reveal the searching which I have in mind. If what is implied is paradoxical, I submit that it is paradoxical not as outraging understanding, but as suggesting at once the nearness and the difficulty of the insight which can surely overtake us if we open our minds to receive it.

In conclusion, however, a rather different issue must be raised. If this article has any single underlying thread, it is a plea for concreteness against abstraction in approach to Christian unity. It would indeed seek to bring the bigoted denominationalist and the 'conference-ecumenical' under the same judgment! But this plea for concreteness demands that we go further. I have already referred to the almost fantastic distortion of contemporary theological activity which the present sterile debate on episcopacy has occasioned. (It would be a moot point whether there is not discernible here a greater *trahison des clercs* than we can see even in the equally obsessive preoccupation of official Anglicanism with canon law revision.) Anyone reading reports of the sort of discussions of episcopacy, ministerial validity and the rest, which go on unremittingly, might suppose that in these matters lay

the central concerns of the faith in this day and genera-
tion. What evidence is there, in an age which is one of
radical unbelief and of profound searching of the foundations, of *comparable* energies being directed towards
fundamental questions of faith and conduct? Or have we
honestly so far retired from the concrete that we suppose,
for instance, the existence and nature of God, the person
of Christ, the possibility of faith, matters secondary in
importance to the precise minutiae of the constitution of
the Church of South India? Or are we in our heart of
hearts so frightened of the tremendous intellectual and
moral efforts involved in seeing, or trying to see, what
becomes of Christian belief as a way of life in 1962 that
we turn, almost in relief, to the parlour games we can
play with our denominational abstractions? Such a question may seem unfair; but some at least of the terms in
which it is cast have surely the unfairness of caricature,
which advertises, by throwing into relief, some features of
its subject. To those who are professionally aware of the
truly searching questions that are being asked of Christians, of the utter precariousness of the structure of belief
by which in some sense they live, there is something
frightening here, compelling even those aware of the
limitations of their own theological perceptions and
knowledge, to prophesy.

We need urgently, all of us, whether Anglicans or non-
Anglicans, new beginnings, I say deliberately *beginnings*.
It is as an element in such new beginnings that in my
view the 'Open Letter' must be judged (it was indeed
because I regarded it as such an element that I signed it).
Its justification lies, in fact, in the future, and it is for
those who signed to ensure that by the way they go from
there they further and do not hinder that validation.

Is Ecumenism a Power Game?

Professor Henderson's book[1] demands to be read, and to be read particularly by Anglicans—whether they be of the establishment south of the border, or of the 56,000 Scottish Episcopalians north of it. They will not enjoy it, they will be tempted to score off it, or to reject it disdainfully as the attempt of the Glasgow Divinity Faculty to make an honest woman out of the *Scottish Daily Express*. But if they resist such temptations, its appearance could well mark a milestone in the history of inter-Church relations in these islands. I am myself a Scottish Episcopalian; and this may explain where I stand. Yet I understand something of what moved Professor Henderson to write as he did; and I want to ensure that his book is taken seriously. Twenty years ago when the news that I was going to the Regius Chair of Moral Philosophy in Aberdeen became known in Oxford, an Anglo-Catholic priest—incidentally a theologian and an exponent of Christian existentialism, not one of the parish clergy—remarked to my wife: 'I hear that Donald is going to keep the light of the faith burning in darkest Scotland.' This remark admittedly is too extreme in its arrogance to need any comment. But I should add that my wife is, and was, a Scottish Presbyterian. There is much to be said on behalf of the Anglican Communion; but there is nothing at all to be said for the attitude illustrated, except to ask whether it is spiritual pride born of ignorance, or ignorance itself born of spiritual pride. Henderson only

[1] *Power Without Glory*, published by Hutchinson, 1967.

glances at the kind of bigotry I have illustrated. The targets of his argument are to be found among the ecclesiastical statesmen and manipulators, one might say among the Annases and Caiaphases rather than among the Pharisees. One of the things that really moves him to fury is the extent to which the manipulators of ecclesiastical influence and power have been able to present Christian division in these islands as something which can be healed by a cunningly devised scheme of integration which turns aside from the frightening depths at which issues of culture as well as of belief have to be acknowledged as pulling men and women apart.

Certainly Henderson underestimates the spontaneous passion for unity that lies behind such gestures as the Nottingham Declaration. But this is partly because in his book he is in fact breaking the strange silence which has prevented the whole issue of Anglican arrogance from being faced openly at all levels—theological, ethical, social, cultural. The example I quoted is only one among very many I could give from a lifetime spent between the two countries of England and Scotland. Such things are part of the built-in inheritance of divisions which are much more than merely theological, and they must be brought right into the open, if union is to be more than something which fairly or unfairly a great many will deeply resent as a cunningly contrived surrender of weaker to stronger, and which in consequence must serve to prevent rather than further that complete mutual acceptance in faith and charity of which it should be the expression.

The time has come when men must stand up and be counted. As one illustration of the sort of arrogance which he seeks to unmask, Henderson mentions in his eighteenth chapter the Tirrell case. This is a matter of fairly recent history in which the project whereby a young American Episcopalian priest named Tirrell, who was pursuing advanced studies at Edinburgh University, would have exercised a full sacramental ministry as an ordained assistant in St Giles Cathedral, Edinburgh, was frustrated by the action of the bishop of the Scottish Episcopal diocese of Edinburgh. Clearly, opinion on the wisdom of the minister's invitation to this young man to assume the position of assistant in the High Kirk of Edinburgh was divided among his Presbyterian brethren. But no one can doubt that the strong opposition to the proposal on the part of Bishop Carey, the Bishop of Edinburgh, played a decisive part in wrecking it. Had he taken a different line the whole matter would have had a different outcome. Of course, the circumstances were complex and confused; in human life they very often are. Yet I believe that Bishop Carey should have taken the risk of giving the young American Tirrell the green light. Whatever the situation, such an action on his part could only have had in the end a deeply healing effect. Certainly Henderson would agree that if Tirrell—still I presume researching at Edinburgh[2]—were now regularly celebrating the Lord's Supper in St Giles, he would have had to write a very different book. I say that, had Bishop Carey acted otherwise, his action would have had a deeply healing effect; and I say this because there is an enormous amount that simply calls for healing—a long history of superciliously arrogant insult, of contemptuous disregard of the claims of devoted men to exercise a true ministry of the Gospel, that Anglicans have to try to blot out, and which they can only begin to blot out by concrete action such as the *encouragement*, not merely the *permission*, to Tirrell to celebrate in St Giles. Henderson repeatedly points out the pathetic arrogance which would query the validity of the orders of a Bonhoeffer or

[2] He has now left that city. (Author's note, February, 1969.)

a Bergrav. By his choice of names he almost makes his readers forget the hurt, borne, I repeat, in strange silence, so often done to lesser men not called upon, as these two were, to face extreme situations, but still never lacking in an ultimate fidelity to the calling by which they believed themselves called.

Henderson, as I say, does not fasten so much on the outrages committed by Anglican bigots, as he does on the pertinacious subtlety of their negotiators—so often, in his view, the superiors in ecclesiastical diplomacy of the men of the Kirk. His book betrays a deep preoccupation with the actualities of power in the ecumenical situation. In his introductory note he admits a debt not only to Gadamer and Jaspers, but also to E. H. Carr, Reinhold Niebuhr and Sir Halford Mackinder. It is these last, he claims, who have helped him to his awareness of the 'power game' that he thinks is being played. And here his analysis, which of course is open to challenge on many points of detail, does suffer from his failure to sympathize sufficiently with the real passion for unity, for the healing of our unhappy divisions, which in the end has undoubtedly inspired the ecumenical movement on the continent of Europe as well as in this country. It was this passion which expressed itself in the Nottingham Declaration ('unity by 1980')—an episode which, I suspect, embarrassed not a few ecclesiastical statesmen. Certainly, Henderson is aware how closely the growth of a decent religious toleration has depended on the acceptance of denominational loyalties as expressive of genuinely conscientious religious disagreements. He has much that is salutary to say on the readiness of ecumenical zealots to identify the goal of their negotiations with the 'will of God', *tout court*. But the impact of his argument would have been sharper had he shown the extent to which the attitudes and policy he detests have drawn their strength from the spontaneous eagerness of ordinary men and women, and not least the young, to have done with 'far off, unhappy things', and find for themselves a newer and more perfect way. Their optimism may be naïve—even slightly pathetic—in its disregard of historical and cultural actualities. But one should hesitate before quenching such a spirit. A Europe that came to know Adolf Hitler had its moments of nostalgia for the hour of Woodrow Wilson.

To say this is not to deny, but rather to emphasize, the importance of Henderson's urgent demand that the ecumenical spends more time in self-knowledge, in getting as far as possible a full purchase-hold on what he, the ecumenical, is up to, on his unacknowledged motives and intentions.

'All power tends to corrupt.' And this goes not only for the more familiar forms of ecclesiastical power, but for the power exercised by the negotiator, by the member of the small élite at the hand-picked conference, suddenly intoxicated by the belief that he is helping under a special guidance of the Holy Spirit to shape the future form of the Church. Moreover, as Henderson repeatedly points out, these things are not done in a cultural vacuum. In the end it is with the faith and Christian practice of simple men and women that these negotiators are playing. In the end, we have to reckon here—and I repeat that I speak as an Anglican—with a deeply searching book with hard lessons to teach us, for all its alternating moods of irony, suppressed passion and sheer rumbustiousness.

The detail of its analysis is, I have said, often open to challenge. Henderson is a man of strong individual convictions; and few, if any, are likely to agree with his every judgment. He is a Scottish Presbyterian, professedly more in sympathy with the 'moderates', with whom in the

eighteenth century David Hume established something
more than a mere *modus vivendi*, than with the 'high-
flyers', qualifying his admiration for the great Dr Thomas
Chalmers with some perceptive criticism. It is enormously
to his credit that in these and other controversial matters
—for instance, the attitude of the Scottish missionaries in
Malawi—he trails his coat openly. His book may distress,
irritate, infuriate; but it has a harsh honesty, and it is
theologically a deeply serious work. I say 'theologically'
advisedly; for throughout it is written as a plea not only
for charity but for theology, for the kind of theology that
demands of the theologian a very hard thing—namely,
the continued struggle for a deeper self-knowledge, for
the kind of theological debate (even with himself) that
the ecclesiastical statesman seems too often to mute.

Henderson brings against the Anglican Communion
the grave charge of attempting a new-style ecclesiastical
imperialism, a take-over bid disguised as a zealous pursuit of Christian unity, but related, of course, to the
eclipse of Great Britain—of that Britain often simply
described as England—as a great power, and also to the
manifestly declining strength of the Church of England.
These charges, as he makes them, need to be qualified.
But they are not groundless (and, I repeat, in this respect
I suspect that for a great many Anglicans, north as well as
south of the border, the Tirrell affair of which I spoke
earlier was a moment of truth, a moment when they had
to ask themselves where their Church really stood, how
far its public face corresponded with its private secret
heart). But what needs, I think, to be stressed is the
extent to which the Anglican approach to these issues
today, on the official level, not only expresses a bland
forgetfulness of the insults of the past but also shows
itself almost incurably intellectually pragmatic, hope-
lessly in bondage to the illusion that it is by the method of

some sort of institutional arrangement that the moral and spiritual hurt of the people will find, if not healing, at least a kind of temporary and possibly permanent anaesthesia. But, as the Professor of Systematic Theology in the University of Glasgow well knows, the age of pragmatism is past. We live in the midst of an overwhelming crisis of belief; and if he is partly justified in emphasizing the insularity and nationalism of Anglican theologians, illustrated sadly by the Bishop of Woolwich's judgment on the work of that magnificently contemporary theological figure, Helmut Gollwitzer, he is also right if he stigmatizes as frivolous the belief that a contrived coming together will somehow solve the testing problems of the possibility of faith.

Henderson says, interestingly enough, very little about the undoubted renewal today of party conflict in the Church of England. Yet one has only to turn to the texts of discussions in Convocation and Church Assembly on prayer book revision to be made aware that the Church of England, and indeed the Anglican Communion, is a deeply divided Church. The term 'comprehensiveness' may be used sometimes not to advertise a source of strength, but to disguise and conceal deep undercurrents of profound, even passionate, disagreement. Initially, within the Church of England this comprehensiveness was secured by the Elizabethan Settlement, which sought through the intervention of the executive to secure a real conformity at the level of religious practice, coupled with a measure of genuine freedom at the level of intellectual opinion. Always at some point the Anglican Communion reveals itself even today as still in bondage to the belief that some such imposed settlement can contain and subdue through enforced adoption of agreed forms of worship (including here the so-called inauguration services of uniting Churches) the stresses and strains of deeply opposed

theological convictions. In the days of Anglo-Saxon industrial and political predominance, with the prestige ac-
cruing therefrom to characteristically English institutions,
there was some possibility of a part of that prestige endow-
ing with its authority the English 'folk-church' (using the
word in Troeltsche's sense). But today we live in a situation in which it is mere dishonesty to pretend that the
crisis of characteristically English institutions does not
infect, and is not in turn infected by, the obvious crisis in
the existence of the Anglican Communion. It is tempting
to turn aside from these realities to the seemingly hopeful
world of reunion negotiations. It is tempting, and, as I
have said, it is in a measure made possible by the eager
passion for unity that Henderson takes too lightly; but it
is escape none the less into a world of make-believe—a
world in which good men incline too easily to think that
they have fulfilled the will of God by ignoring the
realities of history.

In two passages in his book, Henderson touches on the
important topic of the relations between the Church of
Scotland and the tiny, fiercely traditionalist Free Church
of Scotland, standing over against the Kirk in the Highland area. He makes it very plain that part-cause of the
continuing strength of that Free Church in that area
must be sought in the terrible story of the Highland
Clearances. There are those who will write this book off as
the mere expression of Scottish nationalist sentiment. But
how many, one wonders, of those who attended the Holland House Conference could tell of the trial of Patrick
Sellar, to which Professor Henderson refers, and could
dare to suggest—as he does in a very interesting passage
towards the end of the book—that even at this midnight
hour for the Highlands, the Church of Scotland and Free
Church might find a new road to friendship in a resolute
common effort to face the whole issue of the Highland

economy. If Anglicans are to speak with men of the Church of Scotland, they should be reminded of these things, and respect the man who does ask just how they suppose a contrived reunion will serve the cause of flesh and blood humanity in the Highlands and in the Western Isles. There is an earthy quality in this book, an obstinate, attractive awareness of complexities. It will be the greatest pity if its rollicking, slangy method of presentation is allowed to obscure its underlying importance.

I admit I find some of it uncongenial; and I should like to express my deep regret that in the pen picture of the late Professor James Pitt-Watson in the chapter on the Coronation, which mentions his romantic attachment to royalty and his ecumenical ardour, no mention is made of the great courage which he displayed in the autumn of 1956 at the time of the Suez Crisis. In debate in the General Assembly in 1954 he had defended the 'just war' tradition against the pacifists; and when he believed that tradition violated by Anglo-French armed intervention in October 1956, in defence of their alleged rights over the Suez Canal, he said so openly in a way that was certainly costing to one who was temperamentally conservative. While many Christians have used the tradition of the just war as a way of making respectable their adherence to the amoralism of 'my country, right or wrong', Pitt-Watson was not of their number. And though he may have been a little starry-eyed when he went to Westminster Abbey for the Coronation in June 1953, in the harsher hour of 1956 he showed a steadfastness for which many hold his name in reverence. One gathers he did not meet with entire sympathy in the presbytery of Glasgow at that time!

However, I know that by and large I must take Henderson's book seriously, because it is a call to deeper self-knowledge, a call to honesty, even to repentance. He asks for an intermission to all Anglican-Presbyterian conversations in these islands for a quarter of a century; here he is not likely to have his way—and he knows it. But it would be very sad if the grounds of his plea are dismissed as little more than an outburst of bad temper. Perhaps a period of silence would be a good thing, even a period of prayer and a truce to conference. We do not need the bustle of contriving ecclesiastics so much as the recollected silence of men and women seeking to remove from their hearts what stands in the way of complete mutual acceptance.

Ave crux, spes unica. I want to suggest that in the field of inter-Church relations, the fruit of this very simple, very fundamental confession of faith should be found in a readiness to sit down and learn—not to contrive, but to give oneself to learning; to learning of the flesh and blood Christian experience of those within a different tradition from one's own, gladly accepting the opportunity of receiving the sacrament of the Lord's Body and Blood from their ministers. We must bear with them as they are; and their antagonism to our own ethos is something that we must train ourselves fully to understand. We must not suggest that out of contrivance on the part of ingenious and skilful men, devoted to their role but inevitably identifying themselves with it, what may only be won through a discipline of acceptance, through admission of pride and eagerness for power can, by less costing methods, be achieved almost in a few hours. 'It is better to give than to receive.' Who was the wit who said he was glad, as it was certainly so much easier? Can Anglicans learn to receive, not insights simply, but Christian men and women as their teachers of the complexity of the world upon which Christ set the mark of his sovereignty, when alone among the sons of men, himself the Son of Man, he laid all power aside and, at once the

man for God and the man for men, on his cross established that place where past bitternesses are not forgotten
—no, not forgotten, nor overlooked—but made new,
which is very different?

BBC Third Programme, June 1967

The Controversial Bishop Bell

It was to George Bell that in 1946 Dietrich Bonhoeffer's parents gave the copy of the *Imitatio Christi* which had been with him in captivity, in the Nazi prison where the famous *Letters from Prison* were written.[1] A few months before Bell had learnt that he was not—as very many outside as well as within the Church of England had hoped—to succeed William Temple as Primate of All England. On 16 July 1928, a little more than four years after Bell had become Dean of Canterbury, William Ralph Inge had written of him: 'George Bell is a wonderful man. If I were Baldwin, I would pass over all the old bishops and send him to Lambeth. Everyone except Cosmo would be delighted.'

Yet thirty years later, when he died, the man whom

[1] It should be added that at the time this script was written the author had not obtained a copy of Dr Eberhard Bethge's great *Life of Dietrich Bonhoeffer*, published in 1967 in Germany and to appear in due course in English translation; this work contains much extremely interesting material on Bonhoeffer's relations with Bell. While none of this material seems to demand a correction of statements made and judgments passed in the text, it remains true that no one reading Bethge's work can fail to have his sense of Bonhoeffer's great indebtedness to Bell enlarged and deepened. In it we learn also of the extent to which the prisoner whose *Letters from Prison* are now so widely influential was, in the years during which they were written, constantly in the bishop's prayers; more constantly, one suspects, in his mind than in that of any other single person, except the members of Bonhoeffer's own family and those engaged with him in various ways in the struggle in Germany, to which he returned in the late summer of 1939, and in which in the end he met his death.

Inge had thus regarded as already suitable to succeed his former friend and master in the primacy had been for twenty-nine years Bishop of Chichester; the same man who received from Bonhoeffer's family a precious relic of the devotional life of one of the men most surely regarded as formative of the Christian mind of the present age. If Christian faith survives in the twenty-first century, Bonhoeffer, by his writings and by his faithfulness unto death, may well be judged one of the men who made its survival possible. Among his mentors, and his closest friends, was George Bell—a man called to serve as chaplain at Lambeth in the months immediately before the First World War. He was called to serve at a Lambeth whose style and manner he has superbly captured in his own great biography of Randall Davidson: a place utterly different from the Stockholm where he saw Bonhoeffer in 1942, and still more from the Flossenburg where his German friend faced his last ordeal. If you like, Bell bridges the gulf between those two worlds. But he does very much more than supply a formal link between them, establish a sort of ritual continuity between past and present. In his own way, in his own circumstances, he endured the cost of the transition between the two. It was for this reason we may say that Davidson's former chaplain understood Bonhoeffer in some ways much more profoundly than the self-confident *avant-garde* 'non-religious' of today who claim too lightly to be his disciples.

The irony is further deepened when we remember that one of the places in which supremely this depth of understanding was demonstrated in action was the House of Lords. For it was in that setting that Bell delivered his speeches in criticism of the policy of strategic bombing— in that setting where indeed even in the circumstances of 1943 and 1944 they were bound to have a far profounder impact than, for instance, they would have done had they been made at the Chichester Diocesan Conference. As his biographer, Canon R. C. D. Jasper, suggests, these speeches marked a watershed in Bell's career. So much prepared the way for their delivery: the years of ecumenical activity; but also his parochial and diocesan experience, his long and complex involvement in the German Church struggle, even his sense of the establishment of the Church of England as providing a context within which it might exercise a genuinely prophetic responsibility towards the national life. And after the speeches had been given, nothing could ever be the same for the speaker again. The return to Lambeth as primate was simply *out*. But much more than that—the speaker showed himself decisively as the man who had proclaimed the way of the post-Constantinian Church of the future in a setting curiously eloquent of the hopes that first flooded the Christian mind in the remote fourth century. If you like, he tested the moral significance of the Establishment to destruction. Yet of course Bell knew that he was in his action continuing, in a changed context, the witness that Archbishop Davidson had very courageously borne in the same House of Lords in the matter of reprisals for the zeppelin raids of the First World War. Here is a most significant element in historical continuity that one may easily overlook. When all was said and done, Randall Davidson was a great man, with a truly great man's capacity for growth. No one knew this better than his biographer, and perhaps he saw himself at first as doing no more than continuing into the Second World War the tradition his master had established in the First.

But it is with Bell, the man himself, that I am concerned in this talk—even with the deeper cost to himself, because he was the sort of man he was, of the witness he tried to bear. At first sight there is sheer contradiction between his unwillingness to endorse the methods adopted in a supreme emergency to defeat an implacable and monstrous foe, and his early awareness of the depth of evil embodied in the Nazis. Again, in his meeting with Bonhoeffer at Stockholm, he learnt of the beginnings of a conspiracy, which on 20 July 1944 revealed itself to all the world as committed to an act, or indeed to acts, of political assassination. It is not for nothing that Mr R. H. S. Crossman remarked that the only work in the English language really to engage with the moral issues of that plot was Shakespeare's *Julius Caesar*, a work that plumbs to the depths the real ambiguities of political assassination. But Bell had not shrunk, more than two years earlier, from commending this conspiracy at the highest level. Yet deeply aware though he was, before very many in these islands, of the moral and spiritual enormity of Hitlerism, in the anxious days in 1938 between Godesberg and Munich he wrote to *The Times* pleading the cause of settlement rather than justice, emphasizing the small difference between what Chamberlain had accepted in principle at Berchtesgaden and what was demanded the following week on the Rhine. The champion of the German Confessional Church appeared among the advocates of appeasement, at a time when Temple urged Christians to pray for justice rather than peace.

Oh yes! there is contradiction all right. His biographer is right to mention the favourable impression the subsequently convicted murderer, Joachim von Ribbentrop, made on him at their first meeting on 6 November 1934 in the Athenaeum. He was not always by any means a good judge of men; and he displayed on occasion just a little of what Halifax's biographer, Lord Birkenhead, has recently characterized as one of Halifax's besetting weaknesses, an unwillingness to recognize the naked reality of evil. But Dr Ulrich Simon dedicated his sombre, yet profound, *Theology of Auschwitz* to the memories of George Bell and Victor Gollancz. Although Canon Jasper seems to shrink in his biography from presenting Bell 'warts and all', his work is sufficiently minute in detailed information to enable the reader to perceive some of his subject's flaws. We are after all dealing with a human being: one certainly, in my judgment, to be regarded as an authentic apostle, but as such condemned to know the one abiding law of an authentic as distinct from a merely formalized apostolicity—the law summarized by Paul when he spoke of those who were 'deceivers and yet true', and of himself as 'one whose strength was made perfect in weakness'.

Bell saw very clearly the problem of the means—saw the problem with the clarity that only comes to the man who does not simply look on a problem from afar, but who acts in respect of it. Where his judgment on strategic bombing was concerned, he had formidable support in letters from one of the most percipient authorities on strategy and armament in the United Kingdom—Sir Basil Liddell-Hart, a man with a rather frightening capacity for being technically right in his judgments in these fields. Bell did not show himself simply an ecclesiastical jackass intruding on a layman's preserve of which he knew nothing; he showed himself possibly endowed with that kind of intuitive perception which in a democracy is constantly and rightly regarded as a necessary check on the tendency of the experts to assume a kind of moral sovereignty over the man in the street—over those whom Bell called in the doggerel verses he wrote about his career, the 'Nobodies'.

Yet even if the deep encouragement of Liddell-Hart's letters had not been forthcoming, Bell would have gone on—doggedly, obstinately, with that kind of hesitant, almost timid, certainty, at once interrogative and persistent, which is one mark of what may be judged *prima facie* to be authentically apostolic. So in 1943 the Dean of Chichester—A. S. Duncan-Jones, who had in 1938 published with Gollancz a valuable account of the German Church struggle—had to tell him that he would not make a suitable preacher for 'Battle of Britain' Sunday in Chichester Cathedral. And of course there were other weightier consequences.

Canon Jasper's biography is very valuable in that it shows clearly the detail of the life of his subject. If someone goes to his book after reading or seeing the memorable scene in Hochhuth's play *Soldiers*[2] in which the author brings Bell into Churchill's presence to argue the moral issues of the strategic bombing policy, he will feel himself plunged into the world of characteristically Anglican diocesan administration. Of course the European historian will find highly significant material relating to the German Church struggle: but Hochhuth's drama belongs to a different world from, let us say, the problems of ecclesiastical discipline in Brighton in the years following the rejection of the Deposited Book, and the height of the Anglo-Catholic demand for a developed extra-liturgical cultus of the Reserved Sacrament, even from Bishop Bell's later involvement with N. P. Williams over projects of reform in the relations of Church and State in England. These references indeed evoke the atmosphere of the narrower, more specialized, more peculiarly clerical styles of ecclesiastical controversy and excitement. Yet this was part, and an important part, of Bell's world. In a way, indeed, the deep student of his life can trace the continuity between his disciplinary

[2] The German text of Rolf Hochhuth's play *Soldaten* is published by Rowohlt; English translation published by André Deutsch, 1968. See also Appendix, p. 92.

policy where 'Devotions' was concerned, his concern for a measured autonomy for the established Church of England, and the sort of spirituality—I use the word advisedly—expressed and caught in this imagined, yet at the same time deeply informative, confrontation with Churchill.

As I say, Jasper's greatest virtue is in his capacity for retailing detailed information. In terms of personal appraisal his writing has a curiously hollow quality. For instance, his treatment of Bell's marriage and obviously very happy home life, although it is not perfunctory, remains almost conventional. Perhaps where matters so intimate are concerned, this was inevitable. Yet all the time one has the feeling that here is the material for a great biography rather than that biography itself. If you read it, as I did, before reading Hochhuth's scene—and I am talking about this scene in the play: not, I insist, the play as a whole—and then read that scene, you will, I think, be deeply disturbed by the latter; but you will also be electrified. For suddenly in this man, often out-argued, aware of the contradictions in his position, you see someone who out of the assured ambience of the Church of England at its most self-consciously influential came to belong with Dietrich Bonhoeffer—more fittingly laureated with the gift of that surely precious *Imitatio* than with the primatial dignity.

You will be disturbed because Hochhuth makes you feel the ambiguities of Bell's position—its ambivalences, its contradictions; here was this man spared the bitterest experiences of the war, whose objectives certainly included the survival of elementary human decencies, daring to criticize military enterprises more costly than any other in the toll they exacted of precious human lives. The casualty rates in Bomber Command were higher in proportion to the total number of men engaged in its work than that of any other branch of the services. What earthly right had a man living as Bell lived to seem to criticize the men who died as they did? I say 'to seem to criticize'; for he pleads part of the time that he is criticizing not them, but the policies they are implementing: the calculated indifference to the lives of non-combatant men, women and children—non-combatant in the sense in which the aged, the disabled, the six-months pregnant and the unweaned must surely be judged such. And he argues on—stumbling, hesitant, almost regretful. He is nearly defeated in the argument: one senses that he comes to think he has no leg to stand on. It is in his very compassion that he is undermined, by the suggestion that that compassion is born of his relative security from the fearful experience which was the frequent lot of the men who did the actual work in the Hamburg fire-raid of 1943 or the later bombing of Dresden. What right had he to speak of a problem of means? Only the right belonging to a strength made perfect in weakness.

To speak in these terms is not to indulge in a recent, perhaps still fashionable cult of failure or despair. A man's actions are in one respect μιμησεῖς imitations and intimations of his own reality—a reality which is a matter of social inheritance and environment as well as of personal endowment. They are such intimations, and such reflections, even as they also, because they are actions, sometimes profoundly affect the reality from which they spring. So with the witness of George Bell. It was essentially an English, an Anglican, fidelity and it has a great deal of the ambiguity that irritates the more direct Christian spirits about the characteristically Anglican thing. Jasper gives his readers an account of the setting which made Bell's witness what it was: Hochhuth reveals in his fiction something of the cost to the witness, a cost he had to pay in his own Anglican spiritual currency. He did pay it in full: and therefore we call him beyond dispute of apostolic stamp. And of the authenticity of that payment, the gift of Bonhoeffer's *Imitatio* was surely the sign.

But actions do not leave the world as it was: and this, of course, goes for patronage secretaries *et hoc genus omne* as well as for lesser and for greater men. For the Church of England Bell's life is most surely a sign of things already coming upon it. Within the framework of the Establishment—in which for most, though not, I have good reason for saying, all of his life he believed—he heralded, indeed he lived out existentially, the approach of post-Constantinian Christianity. The Dutch Augustinian, Father Robert Adolfs, has suggested that the Church which is coming to be is one that will view the whole history of the Christian Church from the fourth century as a kind of collective experience of the far country in which the prodigal spent his inheritance with harlots.[3] Where the Church of England is concerned, the feel of its peculiar far country may be caught in the Athenaeum rather than in the very different clubs associated with the name of Soho; but the former club is a province of that same delightful, and in the end spiritually destructive land. Although Bell was in a sense always quite at home in that province—he had grown up in it and, to a large extent, he accepted it as relatively excellent—he also knew himself citizen of another country, whose laws and demands were in increasingly sharp conflict with those of the province he knew. The laws and demands were in conflict with the familiar routine—yes—but the content of these laws and demands was far from clear. So he stumbled, even lapsing into the

---

[3] In *The Grave of God: Has the Church a Future?* by Father Adolfs; English translation by N. D. Smith, published by Burns & Oates, 1967.

sad silence of a man defeated in argument. Yet in his apostolate he both achieved for himself a painful self-knowledge, and also by the very sharpness with which he expressed the contradictions of his way, he brought the future nearer. It is for this reason that he is one of the most significant figures in the history of the Anglican Communion in this century; it is for this reason also—and this in the end is much more important—that like Bonhoeffer himself, by his witness he confirmed the weaker, more accommodating faith of lesser men. And if we find him in the end silent, even evasive, are we wrong to hear across the centuries the echo of another inter-rogation—'Answerest thou nothing? Knowest thou not that I have power to release thee and power to crucify thee?' What we cannot speak about that we must assign to silence (to quote Wittgenstein). Yet silence is the most eloquent witness of all.

BBC Third Programme, November 1967

APPENDIX

On Thursday, 12 December 1968, a very effectively abridged English version of Hochhuth's play commenced a run at the New Theatre in London. Those who have seen this version and who have been able to avert their attention, even temporarily, from the author's unfortunate obsession with his (in my view) extremely unplausible solution of the mystery of General Sikorski's death, will recall that in Bell's long and extremely complex argument with Churchill in the third act, the Bishop is finally defeated as a result of his petulant and grossly unfair comparison of a bomber pilot responsible for the death of young children in the Hamburg 'fire storm' raid of 1943 with a pathological rapist who violates a girl of seven in a public park, and afterwards murders her in an effort to conceal his identity. Earlier in the act Churchill had shown himself a man weighed down by the multitude of decisions facing him as supreme executive in Britain's war effort, and oppressed by his sense of the menace of the future; indeed, he had come to the verge of inviting the Bishop's counsel and pastoral help in his genuinely anguished perplexity. But Churchill—knowing the extraordinary courage of the airmen thus criticized, who face a terrible death night after night in the line of combatant duty—is quite properly outraged by Bell's words, and asks him immediately to leave. So the Bishop goes, defeated by his weakness, his mission unaccomplished, even the pastoral ministry Churchill almost invited him to offer in his own deep uncertainties, unfulfilled. It is tragic failure on Bell's part; the flaw in his equipment, namely his inability effectively to sustain an argument in a way at once assimilable by his opponent and profoundly challenging to that opponent's assumptions, is disastrously proved. He is thus thrust back on the μαρτυρία of a powerless silence at a deeper level undefeated, having indeed defined by his protest more poignantly than ever his great opponent's own tragedy. Yet by his acceptance of that failure (an acceptance that acknowledges his own defeat, not that of his cause) he points beyond himself to the sense which for Christian faith is ultimately to be found (in a manner unfathomable to human ratiocination) in the stuff of human tragedy through the *finally* tragic failure of Christ's passion. 'Answerest thou nothing?' Whatever one's verdict on Hochhuth's technical skill as a dramatist, or on the obsession with the Sikorski affair, which obscures his very probing of Churchill's involvement in the bitter dilemma that faced him over Poland, this third act of the English version of his play is ethically and theologically highly significant. It is a comment, achieved through an imagined dialogue between two great antagonists who never thus faced each other, which highlights at once their personal significance and (for the Christian) the deepest lessons to be gleaned from the history of George Bell's apostolate, and which at the same time draws our perception down to the unacknowledged, tragic depths of human existence, where the standards of ordinary moral judgment are not abrogated, but rather turned now one way, now another as the metaphysical import of the issues which engage men and women, and of the men and women engaged by those issues, are partly laid bare. We are deprived of the facile consolation of any sort of 'happy ending' (though we are given practical lessons for the future); but we are enabled to pierce the screen of human history towards the place where its extremities are focussed in a cry for redemption: a cry that is answered not by the advent of a *deus ex machina* but by the coming among men of one 'whom they know not'; whom indeed, when they partly know, they will contrive to destroy, thus not only revealing the lie in their own souls, but ensuring irretrievable disaster for Christ's mission. Yet in this irretrievable disaster is our peace.

20 December 1968